Storealities

by Roquita Coleman-Williams and Other
Empowered Women

The author is grateful
to each of the following contributors
for their permission to print their stories:

Natasha Donerson
Erica Coopwood
Rose Jackson Flenorl
Emily Harvey
Jae Henderson
Natasha Hazlett
Meredith Johnson
Pamela Williams Kelly, Esq.
Nikkya Hargrove
Pat Morgan
Debrena Jackson Gandy
Siobhan Renee Riley
Reverend Marilynn Robinson
Kathryn Vigness
Jasmine "Jaz" Gray
Amy Speropolous
Sherica Hymes
Amy Lorton
Ephie Johnson
Almetria Turner
Mignonne Wright

Printed in the United States of America

Table of Contents

FOREWORD

By Carolyn Chism Hardy

Without pressure, a diamond remains a chunk of coal. Life is the same. We face pressures daily. Each time we meet them with perseverance and courage, we allow a little polishing. And like the diamond, brilliance emerges from the struggle.

Whether you're pursuing a dream or rebuilding your life, you'll go through the process. The polishing is not easy. It requires taking a hard look at yourself. Sometimes it necessitates peeling back painful layers you often prefer to ignore. It may present you with a struggle that begs forgiveness, which you're unsure you can give. Sometimes you must forgive others. Sometimes you must forgive yourself. Polishing demands you hold yourself accountable. It takes courage and vulnerability. It forces you to find the lesson, so your mess can become your message.

The stories in this book are clear examples of this process. Beauty and brilliance have emerged from each contributor's willingness to share her story. And Roquita Coleman-Williams is the perfect curator for this collaboration. She is the master of rising from adversity. Through her strength of character, she persevered through the toughest of times. She sought out educational opportunities to better herself. She broke glass ceilings and emerged an international leader in a male-dominated field.

Roquita's mission is to empower women on a global scale. She walks her talk. Mahatma Gandhi is famous for saying, "Be the change you wish to see in the world." Roquita is a living example of this quote. She locks arms with other women who share this passion for making the world a better place. You will find them among these pages. And you will likely find yourself there too.

Whether you are starting a new business, dealing with the loss of a loved one, living with the scars of abuse or addiction, crawling your way out of a financial hole or facing any of the other pressures that life can throw your way, there is a story in these pages for you. Each woman's story brings you to her place of vulnerability. She will walk you through her journey to the other side. You will discover you are not alone. You are surrounded by generations of powerful women who withstood the pressures to emerge a beautiful and brilliant diamond. Allow them to show you your beauty and brilliance. Read on and prepare to shine.

ACKNOWLEDGEMENTS

"The book you think you will write is not the book you will write." Those are the only words I can really recall from the first meeting with my editor, Mignonne Wright, about this project. We sat in a cozy booth in a bookstore cafe and reviewed the outline for the project. I was excited and overwhelmed. I hardly knew where to begin, but I knew the time had come for me to tell my story.

The project became real when I started writing. I thought the only way I could survive telling my story was to hide behind someone else's name. I created a fictitious name and wrote my story as if I was telling someone else's. When I turned it into my editor, she would not support my "fake name" idea. She explained if I wasn't ready to put my name on it then I wasn't prepared to tell my story. This was far more challenging than I ever imagined. I had to re-write it. She wanted me to put myself out there for the entire world to see. The process was terrifying. In only a few weeks, her words that day in the cafe had become true. And even then, I still had no idea just how accurate they would become.

I decided to make a list of women who inspired me. I knew I could draw courage from their strength. I had no idea so many of these women would end up joining me as storytellers. I could not have predicted the courage some of these women would show as I guided them down the path I had taken. They explored their stories and discovered the lessons they learned in a way that has been life changing to witness. Each of these stories has touched my heart in places that have never been touched. I want to thank each one of these women for entrusting me with some of their most profound treasures.

My husband, Edd, and children Jamie and Kai are my mirrors. These three men cover me with love, support and strength. God couldn't have put more perfect men in my life. My father taught me to expect honesty from men. He never told me a lie. I can say my husband and children are my ultimate truth. They benefit from the lessons I have learned as a woman and are also burdened by those I haven't yet mastered. Any man married to a woman whose light burns bright has to be fire or water. It took three marriages for me to finally understand I could only walk through life honestly with fire.

I want to thank Mignonne Wright for her honesty on the first day of this project. She holds me to my commitment to empower and inspire women. I also want to thank the women in my Growth Mastermind for adopting me as a spiritual sister and teaching what healthy female relationships look like.

Finally, the women in my family have been my ultimate inspiration. Like many families, they are frequently my cheerleaders, competition and critics. No matter which role they have in my life, they have all given me something I needed to get to where I am. In telling my story and hearing the stories of others, I was able to see how truly blessed I have been to have you as my master teachers.

Thank you for the legal counsel and talents of Pamela Williams Kelly, Esq. who ensured every legality was covered to enable a dynamic collaboration with women from one side of the United States to the other.

Special dedication to Dr. Cozetta Shannon "A Felt Brick." You believed in the profound power of storytelling to heal ourselves and help others. There were times in this journey I could feel you guide my heart and hand. We finally got it done my friend.

INTRODUCTION

We all have a story to tell. In fact, we have thousands. Every moment of every day is a new moment, a unique celebration, a new opportunity for growth or heartache. We are all walking motion picture shows; each with a part to play. But one of the greatest things about life is we have the opportunity to choose our role. Or we can give away that right to someone else, and they can choose it for us. For a long time that was my story.

I lived my life for many years allowing others to cast me in my role. The people in my life decided my path and told me how to behave, how to feel, what to pursue and what to leave behind. I was comfortable in this role because it's all I knew. Each day the authentic version of me was silenced into submission. The interesting thing is I allowed it. I played an active role in silencing myself. I lived my entire childhood and a good part of my adult life this way. I didn't understand my womanhood.

It has taken a lot of humility and honesty to tell my story. In my story my fight became surrender. My surrender became my victory.

This book was born from my journey out of the darkness and into the light. On the day I started my journey of embracing and walking in my womanhood, I had no idea where it would lead. I certainly had no idea I was not alone.

So what does all of this mean? A woman accepts her responsibilities. A woman takes ownership of her needs, her desires and her goals. WALKING in your womanhood is much more. Womanhood is your relationship to others. When you walk in your womanhood, you do not minimize yourself for approval. You do not make yourself small to fit into another woman's world. You know you are not above or beneath anyone. When you walk in your womanhood, you need respect as much as you need to give respect. You are authentic. There is no misunderstanding about who you are, what you want and where you stand.

When you walk in the full magnificence of your womanhood, you teach women how to be. They learn this by witnessing your being.

These are stories into the journey of womanhood.

These are the harsh truths we learn on that journey.

The truth: A woman will not support another woman walking in her womanhood if she has not claimed her own.

The truth: You must surrender to your authenticity. You must become victorious in the reality of who you have been created to be.

The truth: The most painful situations are the ones that can show you who you really are.

The truth: You are not alone.

The truth: Someone needs to hear your story so they can begin to heal and embrace their truth.

Each of the stories within these pages is someone's truth. Every contributor is a woman who has inspired me to reach inside and embrace my womanhood. They enabled me to tell my truth. They led the charge to a new way of living.

I hope you learn to examine your own story of womanhood. I hope you rewrite that story in a way that allows you to thrive in your walk with the power you are created to have.

Enjoy-

Roquita Coleman-Williams

Breakthrough

by Roquita Coleman-Williams

I should be thinking about my wedding day. It was only four months away. I should be imagining the smiles, hearing the laughter and anticipating the memories not yet made. The only thing I was focusing on was my breath.

I hid behind my eyelids trying to escape from my reality. Nothing could change the fact that I was in my own personal hell. I knew reality would set in when I opened my eyes. My world was upside down. Instead of planning for my wedding, I was trying to figure out how I got here. What landed me in the hospital for the seventh time? Why had I just had a physically volatile fight with a woman who helped raise me? I needed answers. The level of violence I displayed that day was entirely out of character for me. I had to start digging into my past to save my future.

The hell was one I hadn't created alone, but it would take me going inside of myself to figure that out. I needed to rip up my story like the old carpet in the housing projects where I was born. It was time to find the truth. When I started peeling back the layers, something inside me broke open.

I sat in the hospital bed listening to the beeping of the machines. My blood pressure was 170/110. A bone marrow test determined I didn't have leukemia or lupus. Scans of my brain determined I didn't have a brain tumor. But here I was

2

after an explosive confrontation with a family member. I had an IV in my arm, and the doctor was pushing meds to stabilize my blood pressure.

Relationships I had with some of my family were at the root of whatever was going on with me medically. I couldn't continue to trade dignity and health to honor the sacrifices made for me to overcome poverty.

With a lot of support, I had come out of public housing projects into a beautiful home. I was a marketing executive with a stellar professional reputation. I was well respected in business and as a community leader. In an industry dominated by men, I was breaking glass ceilings.

People relied on me for inspiration and empowerment. When I wasn't mentoring young people, I volunteered with terminally ill children. It would shock people to know I had been in a physical altercation with a member of my family.

I had been in denial about a lot of things. I didn't know myself as well as I thought. I was taking credit for being someone I wasn't. I didn't let that moment define me. I let it give birth to freedom I had never known. I found my truth.

And so we come to the event that changed my life. This moment forced me out of my delusion. I blew up one of the most important relationships in my life. I erupted like the most violent volcano on the woman who helped raise me. That event collapsed my dishonest story into a reality that exploded long before the lava appeared. It is impossible to know when tectonic plates collide. It is impossible to identify the tension that creates a cataclysm that rips the earth apart. How had I missed the pressure bearing in on me with such force that I had erupted so violently, so unpredictably? This was unlike anything I ever thought I would do.

I had taken a break from the wedding plans for a month. But the wedding planner had continued in her commitment. I was sitting at the table looking at all the items she had already sourced for the wedding. I went there to end the business relationship. In other words, I was there to fire her. I immediately began crying as I opened my mouth to speak. This was not just my wedding planner. She was family.

I never wanted to do business with family, but I felt it was my obligation. How would it look? I am an ambassador for economic development in my community. How could I do this and not support my own family business? It felt selfish and hypocritical. But so many issues had come up over the past month. These were deep-rooted family problems I found overwhelming. Now was not the time for me to deal with those issues. I knew terminating the contract for my wedding was not going to be easy.

I initially decided to seek outside support in the wedding plans. But I didn't trust my instincts. Instead, I set my reservations aside. I convinced myself I was a good person and good people always support family. No matter how uncomfortable it might be, it wasn't worth the backlash. Now there was a problem. My wedding planner was doing things that were hurting us and causing a great deal of pain.

My fiancé needed me to stand up for us and our relationship. He needed me to protect him from the chaos going on in my family. I could not stand up for him when the matriarch of my family was the one causing us harm and planning my wedding. I could not focus on my needs or the needs of my husband to be. There were too many outside influences.

I first tried terminating the agreement via e-mail, but that request was not accepted. The wedding planner asked for a face-to-face meeting. I was afraid to have this conversation in person. This was the woman who had helped raise me. I didn't want to look her in the face and tell her I didn't want her to be a part of my wedding. But I could not hide behind a telephone or email. I had to walk in my womanhood and face this.

My voice cracked as I expressed I no longer wanted her to plan my wedding. I wanted to end the business relationship and get out of there as quickly as possible. I was sweating profusely. It was dripping down my thighs soaking the seat of my pants. I kept my hands folded on the table while I inquired about a refund. When she said there would not be a refund, I tore the contract up and told her, "Keep the money. You need it more than I do." I threw the paper shreds at her.

"Be professional, keep your composure, stay polite and polished" was my mantra. I had practiced the corporate walk and talk so long. I had come a long way from the 16-year-old

5

from South Memphis. I wore the labels my family gave as badges of honor—the "dependable one," the "agreeable one," the "easy to get along with" one, the "stay-out-of-drama" one, the "respectful one," the "intelligent one." Where had this aggression come from? Who was this person speaking loudly and disrespectfully to an elder in my family? Who was this person standing in my shoes? Where had she come from? She put her hands on me, and I warned her. This time, when she continued to cross my boundaries, I fought back vigorously.

Who was I fighting? What was I fighting? I wasn't capable of this level of violence towards anyone. But at that moment she became the entire family, and I was battling my history with them all.

I was fighting for my heart.

I was fighting for the baby dropped off to a Memphis housing projects to be raised by a grandmother who struggled with drug and alcohol abuse.

I was fighting for the teenager who was raped during a family trip.

I was fighting for the woman who gave loans to people who talked about me behind my back.

I was fighting for the person who suffered public humiliation at the hands of people who were supposed to love me.

I was fighting for the right to live without their approval.

I was fighting to make decisions based on the needs of the people in my home; my husband, my children and not the opinions of my family.

I was fighting for the young girl who terminated multiple pregnancies between 14 and 20 years old so she wouldn't be the whore they told her she would grow up to be.

I was fighting for the woman who thought the only way I would have a man was by taking care of him financially.

I was fighting for the woman who expected a man to be no more than a good babysitter for his children.

I was fighting for the woman who looked for her father's love in the bed of other men.

I was fighting for the woman who looked for her mother's love in the bed of other women.

I was fighting for the girl who was expected to have the welfare system as her provider and not her husband.

I was fighting for the unmarried teenager who didn't know her child's paternity.

I was fighting for the 4-year-old who needed 15 stitches in her forehead after being hit with a high heeled shoe.

I was fighting against dependence on external validation.

I was fighting against the unrealistic expectations people had of me. I was fighting the judgments I made about them.

I was fighting for the right to be the woman I wanted to be.

I spent years of peeling back the layers of what was given to me without my permission. There was poison poured into my soul, sometimes with the best intentions. What I got was the worst possible outcome. I was still a broken woman and this was proof of that brokenness.

The very first time I walked in my womanhood, it resulted in a physical fight. But I finally stood up for my womanhood. At nearly 40 years old, I was more concerned with how things appeared than how things made me feel. I would leave the powerful, achievement-oriented woman I had become on the work doorsteps. And I walked through my family's doors as a docile girl. I had minimized myself. I dishonored myself. I dishonored them for doing things I hadn't wanted to do.

There was a deep line that ran down the seam of my nuclear family. The line between the intelligent ones and the average ones, six-figure earners and the working poor, international travelers and non-passport holders, the work alcoholics and the narcotic addicted. The most significant line of all, the happy and suffering. I could no longer push down the hurt and disappointment. I couldn't deny the fact I was biologically connected to people who embarrassed me.

Being raped at 16 years old during a family trip to Atlanta had been a secret that I carried with an enormous burden.

Family was involved, and I didn't want to tear my family apart. My grandmother was very protective. The last thing I wanted was for her to be angry with anyone. I wasn't sure what she would do. I never talked about it until the day of the fight. I acknowledged it in the hospital that day after I left my wedding planner's house.

I was raped. The minute I said the words, my blood pressure resumed to normal. No more high blood pressure. No more weird moments of dizziness followed by severe pain in my chests. No more numbness in my arms. I later learned I had been suffering from panic attacks.

It's easier to create a story that focuses only on what was done to you in terrible circumstances. We often take a deep dive into the way in which we were victimized, lied to and mistreated. It is often a lot more challenging to focus on our responsibility in the situation. It's hard to examine how we failed to be our authentic self and to take accountability for our actions. Instead, we need to take life's most devastating times and come out of them stronger. We need to do more than survive. We must thrive. The way you succeed is to be honest about your dishonesty.

The years of suppression and denial caused an eruption. After I erupted, I had to surrender to the truth. I walked away from this fight feeling guilty and triumphant. It was the first time in my experience as a woman I felt whole. There was an eruption of dishonesty that came up in the most violent way as I have ever seen. I masked bitterness with politeness. I concealed rage with accomplishment. I used meditation and yoga to help me keep my composure and hide the pain. Instead, it brought it to surface in a way that I could no longer deny.

I lost that fight.

But I won me.

More in the End

by Natasha Donerson

What in the world should I wear? What's the dress code for this type of thing? In my life, I had many chances to wear the proper outfit. As a corporate executive, I lined my closet with the right suits for negotiating a sale. I wore power suits for the board meetings. I attended them for the various non-profits I worked with on a regular basis. I fought for equality and economic diversity in heels and pinstripes daily. For a wedding, I chose the appropriate dress for the time of the event. If it was a funeral, I wore black.

My life experiences as an entrepreneur with a master's degree taught me how to dress the part. But life had recently taken a drastic turn, and I was standing in my closet completely lost. How do you dress to apply for food stamps? And how did I get here?

Winston Churchill once said, "Success is never final, failure is never fatal." Comprehending this in the middle of the failure is hard.

I couldn't help thinking about the Bible Verse Job 3:25-26: What I feared has come upon me; what I dreaded has happened to me. I have no peace, no quietness; I have no rest, but only turmoil.

I identified with Job because my biggest fear was having no money. This fear always drove me to strive for success on the job, in my businesses, and to take risks investing. My number one goal has always been to make more money. As I hit one goal, I would move the goalpost to make even more. For years, it worked. My bank account always had more than enough to pay bills. I took vacations and invested in real estate and stocks. It wasn't always this way though.

I grew up just above the poverty level. I struggled through four years of college. All the while working two jobs. I received student loans and financial aid to pay tuition. Surviving on a very limited budget wasn't new to me. However, it had been over a decade since I had worried about paying my bills.

Then the tide of success started to change. First, I divorced my husband of nine years. Anybody who has gone through this knows the emotional and financial toll it can take on you. Next, business partnerships went up in smoke. One partner disappeared and left me to pay the bills. My company suffered, and I had to shut it down. Then my real estate holdings started to suffer. I ended up upside down on the properties. Everything happened at once.

To make ends meet I started doing consulting work for a startup company. It meant I could stay afloat by living off my savings and making what little money I could. They fired me on New Year's Eve to save money going into the new year. The consulting work was barely paying the bills. Termination only made my situation worse. I found myself in a terrible depression. I had no savings and less than $500 in my checking account. My monthly expenses were over $6,000 a month. I was broke as well as broken.

It didn't take me long to see I needed to make some tough decisions. As everything was slipping away from me, I was trying desperately to hold on. The first thing I had to let go of was my pride. This led me to my closet trying to figure out what to wear to the food stamp office.

As I pondered how to dress, I thought several times it would be much easier to apply online. Submitting my application online guaranteed no one would see the shame I felt. There was also no chance in hell of someone recognizing me. But I knew I needed help fast! The only way to expedite the application was to apply in person. My mom offered to go and apply for me, but I knew this was something I needed to do myself. I thought there was a lesson in this experience, and I was open to receive it.

I gathered the required documents. I brought my termination letter, my mortgage statement and utility bill. They were already organized in a folder. Two days prior I had made this same attempt and driven to the Department of Human Services Office. I sat in my car for 20 minutes trying to muster the courage to go inside. I got in the extensive line of people flowing out of the entrance and down the sidewalk. People from all walks of life were in line; old and young, black, white and everything between. Most had small children with them. I stood in line and felt like all eyes were on me. After 10 minutes, I returned to my car and went home. I couldn't take it. My shame was louder than the grumbling of my hungry stomach. I didn't feel the relief I was searching for because I didn't know how I was going to buy groceries for the week.

Two days later I was back in line. A little bit of the old me was back and so was my determination. I was mentally prepared. I told myself I was doing research, and this was not happening to me. I pretended I was undercover to do a story I would share one day. I know it sounds crazy, but it helped me get through it. This helped me to realize my circumstances didn't define who I was on the inside.

This time when I arrived, the line was as before if not longer. It took an hour to get a number to be seen by a counselor. Then I had to meet with her to determine if I was eligible to apply. I sat in the crowded waiting room with chairs arranged in rows. The room looked like a huge open auditorium. Before long a pre-screening counselor called me. She reviewed my documents and assigned me to caseworker by issuing me another number. I went back to waiting again.

My caseworker, Donald, called my name a little while later. He was a young African American male in his mid-20's. At his cubicle, he had a picture of his wife on his desk. He smiled when he shook my hand and told me to have a seat. I still remember his puzzled look when he looked at my application. He noted my mortgage payment and the type of car I drove. Then he looked up and said, "So you have   a master's degree?" Impressed but also confused, he wanted to know how I got in this situation. After our fifteen-minute interview, Donald determined I was eligible for SNAP benefits. He said I would receive my benefits in five days, which meant my situation was urgent. It usually takes 30 days. He approved me for three months. After three months, I would have to provide updated documents to continue. But I knew that would not be necessary. Since I found my determination, I made a vow to be off assistance by then. I didn't know how, but I knew I would be in a better place. Call it faith or eternal optimism, but I was right.

Applying for government assistance to feed my family was rock bottom for me. When things seemed to get better, something would happen to remind me my situation was the same. For example, one day I received a contract for a small consulting job. A few days later I got the notice one of my tenants was being evicted for nonpayment. I also found out the rental house needed thousands of dollars in repairs. My mother gave gave me money to pay my car note. Then I found out I needed new tires because they were no longer safe to drive. Bills, foreclosure notices, and IRS letters flooded my mailbox daily.

I was grasping to hold on to all the material things that were weighing me down. One day my attorney asked me a simple question. "Why are you trying to hold on to all these investment properties when they are not paying the bills?" I didn't have a response. Five minutes passed by. She looked up from my file and said, "I'm still waiting for an answer" I finally responded with "I don't know" as I burst out crying. Then I had an epiphany. I was holding on to the properties because of what they represented. To be able to say I have over ten investment properties made me feel wealthy. It didn't matter if they were upside down in market value and not covering the mortgage payments. I was holding on to the facade of success by going through all my savings and my retirement account. I was trying to stay afloat even though I was sinking deeper and deeper into debt.

I decided to get my head out of the sand. Standing straight, facing forward with my eyes open, I had to accept my losses. With acceptance came the lifting of the weight and a clear view of how to start over.

I didn't allow the brief occurrences of despair to linger long. On days I wanted to cry and feel depressed, I would set the timer on my phone for thirty minutes. Then, I would lie in my bed and think about everything and cry my eyes out. After I heard the chimes on my phone, I knew thirty minutes had passed. I would get up, wash my face, and find something positive to read. The tears were a cleansing for my soul that allowed me to embrace a new outlook.

As I searched for jobs, I read inspirational books throughout the day. I studied successful people. I read biographies of famous people who had failed several times before hitting it big. Whether it was a documentary, magazine article, or book, I read every comeback story I could find. Reading about other people was all the proof I needed. It helped me to know my current situation was a setup for greater things to come. It was important for me to feed my mind with positive images that created feelings of prosperity. The result was an incredible sense of faith.

I am better in so many ways because of the experience. Fear no longer drives my decisions or goals. I experienced my greatest fear of going broke. Then I recovered. I have more courage now. Even if I lost it all again, I know what to do to gain it all back. There is no fear in what could happen. I know to make better decisions. I have faith everything will work out in my favor in God's timing.

What I lost in currency, I made up in personal relationships. My mother and aunts provided the emotional support I needed. They also helped financially. I now have daily phone conversations with them. The extra time we spent together because I needed a hug will be cherished forever.

I also formed new friendships with women who provided much wisdom and encouragement. They helped me see what was to come and to know the despair I was feeling was temporary. The love and support from my family and friends were more significant than my financial situation.

Three months to the day after I applied for government assistance, I landed a long-term contract. It paid more annual income than I had ever made before. The properties I kept no longer had vacancies. After paying the mortgage and expenses, I was profitable again. It was the shift I had been waiting for and expecting to happen.

Going back to the story of Job in the Bible, it's easy to focus on how much he lost. Later I meditated on how God blessed Job with twice as much as he had before his trials began. His faith was rewarded. So was mine.

Winston Churchill also said the only thing that matters is courage. I succeeded, but it wasn't final. My downfall was not a failure. It took courage to walk into the reality I was living and embrace it. I didn't let it destroy me. And I am better for it!

Let Peace Be Your Umpire

by Erica Coopwood

All my life I had a clear vision of where I was headed. I knew what I wanted to do. I knew where I wanted to go. And as I walked my path with a clear focus on my future, I prayed to God each step of the way. So how did I end up walking out on my dream at the very moment I was finally reaching all my goals? How did I end up feeling defeated when I should have felt victorious?

Let me explain. I decided at nine years old to write down my goals. Growing up in the Delta, in Yazoo, Mississippi I knew I would need a plan to make my dream of becoming a lawyer come true. I would have to figure out how to get a scholarship because my family would not be able to pay for all of my schooling or send me to college. I made a list on an old poster board left over from a school project. Work hard, study, get the best grades, get a scholarship, graduate. Also on the list was my desire to work for a large law firm in the downtown area of a large metropolitan city. I wanted to live close enough so I could still come home to see my parents. Yes, at nine years old I wrote it all down.

Year after year, with the good Lord's help, I checked each item off my list. When I got my job in downtown Nashville, Tennessee, I knew I had arrived. I got married to a man, a widower, with three smart young boys. I had a daughter and continued to fill in each checkbox as the days went by. I had done all I set out to do. Then it happened.

I was lost in the case file for one of my clients, and I heard God ask me, "Are you happy now?" I stopped. I looked up to the sky and let his question sink in. I was confused. It wasn't supposed to be about happiness. I was so focused on checking off the boxes in my life I didn't stop to ask if this was what God had planned for me. So I was surprised to hear his question. I pushed it aside and kept working. It didn't make sense to me. I spent my entire life working to be a lawyer and here I was. I ignored him.

Sometime after that day in my office our nanny, Ms. Doris, gave me another nudge. We were open and honest with each other, and because of this relationship, she felt compelled to have a word with me. I will never forget the words she spoke. Ms. Doris said, "I love the money you are paying me to keep your baby. Lord knows I have so many projects around my house that need doing, and it helps pay for all them. But this is not right." She explained, "You are spending too much time working on other people's problems and where you want to be is here." I didn't react at the time. I said, "Ok" and told her I would think about what she said.

I was raised by a mother who at one time had three jobs and was rarely at home. She was sixteen when she had me, so we grew up together. She was a nurse, and my grandmother was a nurse. My grandparents raised me. I remember my grandmother working night shifts and carrying me to our neighbor's house, Miss Emma. My grandfather was the best man I've ever known, hands down and rest his soul. But back in those days, you knew better than to leave a girl child home with a man. So off to my neighbor's house I went.

My mother lived in a different city, so I knew what it was like to grow up in a home without the regular presence of my mother. I didn't get to know her. So, this perspective touched a nerve with me. When I got married, my husband had three little boys who lost their mom. They had grandmas and aunties, but they didn't have a mother figure. I considered this as well. But I continued to go to work every day and continued to check off the boxes. God started steering me in a completely different direction.

This is how He works; softly and gently. Just a nudge here and there to get you to think. Between the words from God in my office and the words of Ms. Doris, my mind started to work overtime. His gentle prodding started working on me. In His infinite wisdom, He knows me inside and out. He knows what it takes to get me to listen. But still, I ignored the nudges.

That's why I never saw it coming. I had planned my whole life to reach this point. When it all went away, I didn't even realize it was happening. It took heartache to make me listen in the end.

One day my plan was in place and just 24 hours later, it was gone. The life I planned came to a screeching halt!

I found myself in an extremely volatile working relationship with one of my superiors. My dream became a nightmare. It was awful. Day after day it got worse. When I finally decided enough was enough, I didn't tell anyone there about my decision to leave. On my last day my husband helped me pack up my office. Out the door I went. Although it was out of character for me to walk away, I was so disheartened because the work environment was too ugly. Like I said, He knows me well. This was the last push I needed.

What happened next was not on my checklist. But it was on God's. Jeremiah 29:11 reads, "For I know the plans I have for you," declares the LORD, "plans to prosper you and not to harm you, plans to give you hope and a future." I thought my future was at the top of a corporate ladder. For a young woman who had her life all mapped out it was hard to see what His plans were for me.

I walked away from that law firm. I wish I could say I never looked back but I did. There were times I longed to be the lawyer at the top of my game, solving the puzzling lives of the firm's corporate clients. But I am a follower of God. He led me away from my plans and into His. When I felt confused and lost, I had to have faith. When I got frustrated and angry, I let peace be my umpire. In time He revealed His plan. The life I ended up with was far different from the life I expected.

He sent me signs to guide me towards His path. Ms. Doris was one of those signs. He challenged me to consider what real happiness was. Then He showed me. He led me to play a role in my family I didn't know they needed. He wanted me to focus on being a wife and a mother. That is not His desire for everyone, but it was what He wanted for me. He knew the plans He had indeed. For this, my life is blessed in ways I could never have imagined.

Have A Goal

by Rose Jackson Flenorl

I can still feel the sun's warmth across my face on that summer day. I rode in the car alongside my daddy as we were leaving my grandparent's home. We were heading back to our hometown of Clarksdale, Mississippi.

As we continued on that long narrow road, I saw a little sundry with the words ice cream printed in bold letters. "Daddy, I want an ice-cream cone," I said. He pulled up to the sundry, got out of the car and asked to buy his child an ice-cream cone. The attendant was harsh and told him he didn't serve black people. As a small child, it was painful to see my Daddy treated this way. He climbed back into the car, and we left without an ice cream cone. From that experience, I learned there were barriers we needed to break. It was only later I realized I could be a force for positive change if I dreamed big and set goals.

Fast-forward to the beginning of my freshman year at Ole Miss. This was a time when minority students were only about six percent of the student body. I had graduated from Mississippi's Clarksdale High School. I was the first African-American valedictorian at the school. I was excited about starting college and discovering new pathways.

I was hanging out with friends in the student union when I noticed pictures on the wall. They were of outstanding students who had graduated in the Ole Miss Student Hall of

Fame. These students being singled out as seniors amazed me. They received the university's highest honors and went on to be great leaders. They represented so many different fields. They were now in education, government, business, law, journalism, ministry, sports and entertainment. The faces on the wall included Archie Manning (NFL Football Quarterback), William Winter (58th Governor of Mississippi), Robert Khayat (former Ole Miss Chancellor), Jake Gibbs (Major League Baseball Player), Jimmy Autry (President of Meredith Publishing) and many more.

As I gazed at that wall, I said aloud in front of my friends, "What if I could graduate in the Student Hall of Fame?" I heard laughter. Loud, shoulder-shaking laughter. And then I heard words I'll never forget.

"Do you see anybody on that wall who looks like you?" The laughter continued. My eyes went from that wall to the floor where I stared in humiliation. What had I done? Did I just share an impossible dream out loud? Would others think I thought I was better than everyone else? How long would they be laughing at me?

I got up and headed to my dorm room in Hefley Hall, crawled into bed and cried like a baby. It was one thing to be discouraged from pursuing a dream; it was another to be laughed out of the student union.

When I finished my pity party, I began my soul-searching: "Why did you come to this college?" I asked myself. "Are

27

you going to let naysayers slay your dreams? Do you have the faith to pursue your dreams?"

I shifted gears and started digging for data. I wanted to find out as much as I could about the selection process for the Student Hall of Fame. I had no internet, Google or Facebook. I found the Mississippi Room in the library and launched my research campaign. I reviewed old yearbooks and student newspapers. I discovered Ole Miss had been inducting students into the Hall of Fame since 1930. They based the selection criteria on the student's academic achievement. They also considered their leadership and community service experience. Finally, they measured the students' potential for future success.

Most of the students had been leaders of student organizations or athletic standouts. Some were community leaders. I then began researching student organizations to learn their requirements. For the first time in my young life, I wrote down a goal and the steps needed to reach my goal. I had a plan.

During my freshman year, I would join a student organization. My sophomore year, I would chair a committee. My junior year, I would run for an office. I would put in the hours needed to be successful academically. I would pour my heart into community service and help others. I made peace with myself. I decided even if I didn't end up in the Hall of Fame, it would be OK. I would still have leadership skills, good grades, and lifelong friends. I will have given my time and talents in service to others. In essence, I'd be the best Rose God created me to be.

So what was the outcome?

In my senior year at Ole Miss, I became the first African-American female inducted into their Hall of Fame. My picture is on that wall. The little girl who didn't get her ice-cream cone because of her skin color is now on the wall of one of Mississippi's most powerful institutions. I had broken a barrier – not only for myself, but others.

Valuable lessons paved that long road from the ice-cream sundry to the Student Hall of Fame. I learned there's an activist in each of us and all we have to do is exercise our power to act. I learned the importance of dreaming big and not allowing naysayers to slay our hopes. I learned to identify a goal, write it down, and bolster it with a solid plan. I learned to stand on my faith in good times and tough times.

Yes, we all love the thrill of beating the odds and winning. But I've also learned the real test of our character and strength often comes when we fail.

I decided to try and break another barrier during my senior year by running for Miss Ole Miss. My campaign slogan was "Pick a Rose for Miss Ole Miss." I had a dedicated campaign team, and we ran a good race, but I lost. Running for Miss Ole Miss was also the first time I experienced overt racial comments. I found racial slurs scribbled across my campaign signs. Many people told me the state of

Mississippi was not ready for an African-American Miss Ole Miss. When I worked toward the Hall of Fame, my personal goal was not on public display. Running for Miss Ole Miss put me out front and center. This was a fiercely competitive campus-wide campaign. I had to come face-to-face with hurtful tactics. Somehow I still had to maintain my dignity and composure.

From this loss, I learned a valuable key to success is not to let failure defeat you. I aimed high and missed. At least I took the shot and showed others sometimes having "guts" is greater than getting the "glory."

The chance you take may break down a barrier for those who come behind you. The Hall of Fame wall at Ole Miss , in Oxford, Mississippi, now has a lot more pictures that look like me. Little did I know my hard work would create a path for my daughter Lillie. Her picture is now up there with mine. Within each of us is a triumphant spirit awaiting its' time to arise, shine and teach.

Make a Call

by Emily Harvey

I was wearing a pink dress covered in ladybugs. I matched the new pink phone booth outside in the garden purposely and perfectly. As I stood before the dozens of people gathered in the pews before us, I wept for the first time in months. Like rain, tears fall when they decide to. And in that moment, they fell because what I had accomplished. I knew then I could do anything. I stood at the pulpit holding hands with my friend, a recovering heroin addict on one side and my pastor on the other. Our heads bowed in prayer.

Two years earlier at the funeral home, I gazed up at an oversized portrait of my boyfriend in a gaudy gold frame. His mother was kneeling on the floor, sobbing. My family had been the first to arrive. I could barely walk, much less mingle. His mother sensed someone nearby and turned around. She stood up as I moved closer. She held my shoulders, looked me in the eyes, and said, "He loved you more than anyone in the world." We hugged each other, crying. I handed her a photo of her son and me from a wedding we had attended together. She glanced at the picture, but it made her cry more. By that time, other friends and family started to arrive, and I moved aside. I couldn't stop shaking. My sister and my mom walked me to the car, and went home.

I lost a part of myself that day. Our codependency became clear to me after his death. I struggled to find the conviction to take part in everyday life. I stayed in bed for months. I watched entire seasons of mindless TV shows. I accepted whatever drugs and drinks were around to forget reality. Numbness was the only goal. No progress, no movement, no growth, no emotion. I moved back home and into my mom's house a year later. Feeling sorry for myself, I did nothing to help others. I still had so much I wanted to say to him, but he was gone. I had relied on him for approval and affirmation for years. Now, I had to find out who I was without him.

A year after his death, the report confirmed my suspicion. He died of a heroin overdose. He had tried heroin in the past, but the desire to use does not go away. I thought we told each other everything, but he kept this secret from everyone — even me. I remember one instance in the spring before he passed away. It was allergy season, and I was sneezing a lot that day. Suddenly, his nose started bleeding. He said, "Oh, my allergies are so bad!" Later, I learned he was snorting heroin. I was naive about his drug use. I didn't see the warning signs; the increased secrecy, dilated pupils, nosebleeds, track marks, stomach pain and mood swings.

Around 18 months after his death, I heard a story on NPR that caught my attention. It was a story on This American Life about a man in Northeastern Japan who built a phone booth in his garden. He used it to feel connected to his cousin who passed away. A few months after he built the phone booth, a tsunami devastated a town nearby named

Otuchi. Thousands of people took a pilgrimage to visit the phone booth. They came to "whisper" messages to their lost family members. The creator, Itaru Sasaki, a 70-year-old gardener, called his phone booth the Phone of the Wind. It is a simple rotary phone housed in a white phone booth. It looks across a romantic garden and the Pacific Ocean. The spiritual principles of reincarnation and ancestor worship brought magic to his phone booth. The radio story included visitors talking to their lost loved ones. They were telling them simple happenings in their life. The conversations helped them feel connected to them again.

My ex-boyfriend and I had spoken regularly on the phone over a two-year period. I related to the people in the story longing for an avenue of connection with their loved ones. As I listened, I felt called to set up a similar booth to help myself heal as well as my friends and neighbors who also had to say goodbye to their loved ones too soon.

I recognized hope for the first time since his death. I found a way to help people who felt the same grief I did. After a quick search, I found a phone booth for sale on Craigslist. It was only 20 minutes outside of town, and the phone was the perfect shade of pink. I knew it was my booth.

I went with my family to check out the booth. It needed some deep cleaning, but that didn't stop the project. It is about seven feet tall, a few feet wide and has clear glass windows on all sides. In the corner sits the light pink phone, and to dial a number, the caller spins the dial in a circle to the bottom. Across from the phone was a seat with fabric dating back to the 70s. The brand is Benner-Nauman. They were a popular company making the majority of phone booths on the west coast in the 1960s and 1970s. I told the seller to give me a few months to find a home for it.

Soon after visiting the booth, I pitched my idea to my Church Council. They agreed to give my booth a safe space in the community garden. There were several things we had to do to prepare for the installation. We dug a square, poured concrete, and had the phone booth delivered. We gave it a thorough cleaning inside and out. We replaced the seat cushion and added a pink leather-bound guest book. The guest book includes my personal story. It also has resources for addicts and friends of addicts. There are extra pages so visitors can write a message when visiting the booth.

I named the phone booth The Phone of the Spirit and, in 2017, I hosted a dedication ceremony. At the ceremony, a recovering heroin addict told her story. She spoke of hope and change, her three overdoses, her recovery, and her son. Now she is in school studying to be a social worker to help other addicts.

The phone booth is now open to the public. It is used as a sanctuary for grieving, praying and quietly communicating. Wind does not carry the messages to our loved ones. Prayer is what powers this phone booth. Prayer lifts our words to the departed. It helps us feel connected to them through the Holy Spirit.

In learning to grieve the loss of my former boyfriend, I found the hope of recovery through helping others. By setting up the phone booth, I have been able to share our story. I can raise awareness about the heroin epidemic across our country. I have seen stories help people who are grieving the loss of loved ones from an accidental overdose. Now I know he kept his drug addiction a secret from me so I would not get addicted too. I am confident I was saved from the fate of heroin addiction so I can help others.

The Phone of the Spirit is in the community garden at St. John's United Methodist Church in Memphis, Tennessee. It is one of the most beautiful gardens in the city. The community can visit the phone booth any time to say things left unsaid to lost loved ones — even a simple hello. I invite you to visit this quiet space, dial in a prayer and send it to the sky.

Beautiful, Happy & Blessed

by Jae Henderson

"Why are you so hard on yourself? Even with awards and honors, you never felt good, intelligent or deserving enough."

How was she able to recognize the gifts in everyone else but not acknowledge her own? Why did she give compliments and encourage others but could not affirm herself? This woman was a real contradiction. This woman was me. Sadness and low self-esteem cloaked me like a winter quilt. I couldn't shake it. After a while, I didn't try to mask it with a smile anymore. Instead, tears were my companion. What was wrong with me? Why didn't I like myself?

Then one day, while in college, I met a man. Not any man but THE MAN. He was a handsome, kind and compassionate college student. He stared at me as if he were examining me, looking through a glass box with self-loathing folded inside. It made me uncomfortable. I tried to look away, but he cupped my chin and guided my gaze back in his direction. "You're beautiful," he said to me. I laughed and thought to myself that he couldn't be talking to me. How could he say that? I was skinny—about 110 pounds with small breasts, no booty and no hips. I didn't believe him. He was my boyfriend and biased. Wasn't he saying what boyfriends are supposed to say? Across the campus were women with bodies like celebrities in music videos. These were the women I believed deserved the gaze of a handsome man. At 20 years old, I could pass for a 16-year-old. What could he see in me?

When I looked at myself, all I could see were flaws. One of my front teeth protruded forward more than the other and my nose was too broad. I didn't believe I was beautiful so how could anyone else? But the next day and every day I saw him after that, he reminded me, "You're beautiful." It took a while, but the moment came when I stopped trying to turn my head as he gazed at me. I didn't laugh anymore or question why he saw me as he did. Instead, I listened. He met me as a girl who had not learned to love herself. But now I was learning to appreciate myself and the story behind every part of me. My appearance didn't change. My nose was still wide but now it was a gift I inherited from my grandmother. I still had one tooth that jutted out a bit too much but it was part of my beautiful smile and perfect all the same. I finally felt happy, beautiful and blessed.

Then, our relationship ended. When I realized what we had was gone, I thought we made a tragic mistake. I suggested we try again but the damage was done. Too much pain was inflicted on both sides. The love we had left didn't feel like it used to feel. It was over. As I looked at him with tears in my eyes, he said, "You're stronger than you think you are." Initially, those words stabbed me like a thousand daggers because in my mind being with him gave me strength. I felt better about myself because I was loved. As the days passed, and the healing process took place I realized he was right.

With or without him I was going to be okay. I had to get to that place of authentic acceptance and love for myself. In order to do that I had to take another look at the path that led me to a place of self-loathing.

When I was young, no one told me I was pretty. I wasn't physically developed like my high school friends. There were no shopping sprees to grab the latest fashions. I didn't have weekly beauty salon appointments for my hair and nails. I had a simple press and curl done over my mother's kitchen stove. I didn't live in a big house, in a suburban neighborhood and my mother didn't drive a nice car. In fact, by the time I reached college the only car she owned sat dormant and rusting in our front yard. I coveted what other girls my age had and resented my own life. It would take finding love and losing it for me to explore the beauty in circumstances I once loathed.

I wasn't belittled as a child or told I was ugly. I was well cared for, taught good life principles and loved by my family. Measuring my life to others was the wrong way to determine my value. I got an accurate reading of my worth once I realized that. I rise to good health and loving friends and family. I have a job I enjoy, a house I call home and I thank the good Lord for my life. I am strong, bold and beautiful. Although I've worked hard to make sure the world knows it, more so I know it.

Today, when I see a little girl, I tell her she is beautiful. Because I know we need to hear certain words to know it for ourselves. When the right words are not said, it can hurt as much as when the wrong words are said. Even now as a woman in my 40's I struggle with self-esteem. But I know how to better manage those "I don't like me moments." I have confidence. I know who I am and what I bring to the table. I realize if good things are going to happen I have to take steps to make them happen. I fashion my happiness from the wise decisions I make and only allow people to stay in my world who add value to it. I work hard to keep this world I've created intact. And my happiness is not dependent upon any man who may come into my life. I've reached a point where I can recognize I am beautiful, happy and blessed. I no longer need anyone else to show me.

The next time you look at yourself in the mirror and you don't like what you see, I want you to do something for me. Loudly proclaim these words, "I am smart. I am strong. I can achieve anything I put my mind to for I am fearless and I'm beautiful." Keep repeating them until you believe it. I fell in love with a handsome young man who helped me take the first steps on the journey to loving me. His presence and his absence both held valuable lessons. People come into our lives to help build our foundation. But writing our happily ever after is our own responsibility.

One Decision

by Natasha Hazlett

By most people's standards, I was at the top of my game. I retired from my full-time law practice at the age of 33. I had a fantastic husband and beautiful one-year-old daughter. Together my husband and I had an international marketing training & consulting company. We ran it from our laptops while living in the gorgeous foothills of the Rocky Mountains in Boise, Idaho.

Years ago I felt "called" to quit my law practice. I needed to empower a group of entrepreneurs who would be beacons of light in the darkening world. I accepted the call, pushed through my fear and quit my job.

I'm certain people envied our freedom. Our life. If only they knew what was going on behind the curtain. Behind the perfect Facebook pictures.

Behind the curtain, I felt, mentally and physically, like a hot mess. I remember one afternoon in particular, just like it was yesterday. I leaned against the kitchen counter and sobbed to my husband, "I want to walk away from EVERYTHING. I don't want to coach my clients. I don't want to teach another web class. I don't want to inspire anyone! I need to go back to my job. That's it!"

"But what about your calling?" Rich asked. He knew this was the ONE thing that would USUALLY snap me out of my funk.

"God picked the wrong damn girl for the job!" I whimpered through the tears.

The week following my kitchen-meltdown wasn't much better. I felt like a zombie. I wasn't inspired. I felt empty. I had nothing left to give anyone. I had nothing for my husband. Nothing to offer my clients. Nothing to give my friends. What little I had, I gave to my little girl. I waited seven long, painful years for her precious soul.

"What's wrong with you?!?" shouted the voice in my head. "You have what you want...what else is there? Don't be selfish. Get your shit together."

But I couldn't. I couldn't do it anymore.

Another week went by, and I was faced with a decision. We had already purchased tickets to attend a business conference in San Diego, and it was game time. Would I give up the tickets, the money for the plane ticket and hotel room...or would I suck it up, and go?

I knew if I wanted to even have a CHANCE of getting myself out of this hopeless funk, I had to go to this event.

After all—Marcus Lemonis, one of my all-time favorite TV business mentors would be there.

On nothing but a wing and a prayer, I packed my bags and headed to San Diego for the 3-day conference.

The first two days sparked a little fire within me that was snuffed out by the end of the day. As I started Day 3, I had only the tiniest shred of hope left that the inspiration I was seeking would appear. It looked like I was headed back to my job and admitting defeat as an entrepreneur.

Then out walked Marcus Lemonis—the last speaker of the event. He asked the audience one simple question: "What's one thing that you've never told anybody and how is it affecting your business?"

In that moment, surrounded by 1500 strangers, the answer washed over me.

"I hate myself."

There. I said it.

I hate myself.

When I looked at myself in the mirror, I hated the person staring back at me. Hated her. This hatred was most undoubtedly fueled by the 55 pounds I had gained over the past seven years.

There were other contributing factors, but this was the biggest. "Now," I thought... "How did that little gem affect our business?"

The answer was as plain as day: It was the sole reason our business hadn't grown over the past three years. I didn't feel worthy enough to inspire and to lead others. I felt like a complete fraud. If anyone knew, they wouldn't want to learn from me, much less do business with me!

So I refused to create content my audience would love. I refused to take on the projects when my husband asked me to help. The sad reality was I was the flat tire on our bicycle. I was making my poor husband peddle for the both of us while bitching about how slow we were going.

That epiphany was just the beginning. Marcus spoke about the importance of reinvention in life and business. My truth continued to wash over me. The little voice within me finally allowed me to see my reality in a way I had never seen before.

It turns out the fat I piled on my body was all a physical manifestation of the hatred I had for myself. The extra pounds represented the hate I had for the fact I was infertile. The hatred I had because I wasn't as skinny and pretty as some of my competitors in the online business world.

Marcus was continuing to talk in the background. At that moment surrounded by 1500 strangers, light and truth-filled me. The clarity of my reality became a huge blessing to me. I seized that precious moment and made a straightforward decision. I wanted that fat/hatred gone. Now.

I wanted to LOVE myself. I wanted to be the REAL and authentic me. Not the person that cowers behind bars of chocolate and glasses of wine and pints of ice cream. I wanted to step out and shine.

For the first time in years, I felt alive. I felt light. I felt infinite joy. I knew where I was headed; a complete and total reinvention. I knew my first step.

As I sat on the plane waiting to take off for Boise, I pulled out my iPhone. I typed a message to the hard-core nutrition coach I had been thinking of contacting for months.

"Ok Cristy—let's do this thing. After what seems like a lifetime of self-sabotage with food—I'm ready to shed the pounds and step into the woman God wants me to be. What's the next step?"

At 8:30 AM the next morning, I walked into Cristy's office. I broke down in tears as I shared with her my journey to becoming clinically obese. Then, I handed over a check. I congratulated myself on taking the all-important first step of my reinvention. Over the next 5½ months, I shed every single one of those 55 pounds of hatred.

When I look in the mirror now, I see a woman whose light shines brightly. All it took, was one decision.

My journey reminds me of a quote by Jen Sincero, author of "You Are a Badass." "It's not your fault that you're [messed] up, but it IS your fault if you choose to stay [messed] up."

I chose to walk away from the mess. I decided to shed the ugliness of my past. I decided to reinvent myself, and because of that brave decision, life got a whole lot sweeter for me.

Clients started coming to me in droves…not just any clients-PERFECT clients. I was a happier and more joyful wife, mother, coach and friend.

I walk with a pep in my step and confidence I never knew existed within me. I am living on purpose and with purpose.

Some may think reinvention is a bad thing...it isn't. It's a badASS thing.

Friends, you are in the driver's seat of your life. YOU. Not your mom, your dad or your significant other. Not your kids. Not the ghosts of your past.

Not the same BS stories you've told yourself about why you aren't living the life you imagined. You can have everything you want in life—you can make the impact you are intended to make... ONE decision is all it takes!

There's Something Wrong with Her

by Meredith Johnson

Journal Entry

January 30, 2006

I HAVE MY LIFE BACK,

AND IT IS BETTER THAN EVER!

I love life, especially mine. I love everyone! I even have a secret crush. The boy who was teasing me in class before admitted he was only trying to get my attention. We spent an hour on the phone talking about my idea for my senior presentation. Then, I explained my depression, which led to my current blooming transformation.

He's actually a wonderful person.

I LOVE my school, class and life.

I have been BURSTING with creativity lately. I love myself again! I'm writing up a storm and so excited about my projects at school in art and history.

Before writing the journal entry above, I had been suffering from seven months of debilitating depression. Then an intense change overcame me. While drunk at a Christmas party, I exclaimed, "I don't want to be sad anymore!" I thought I had somehow cured myself. I hadn't. But there was a crucial change...although we didn't realize it yet. Mom felt relieved I wasn't depressed anymore. However, now she and countless others worried about something else; something even more threatening.

During our soccer team's Senior Night game, I scored a lefty goal. I was yelling at my teammates during the game and sprinting faster than I ever had. I felt like Superman. The other team stared at me in a quandary. That same night, I attended a Mardi Gras Ball with some alum friends. I got rip-roaring drunk pre-gaming before we even left. I hadn't eaten anything but an apple that day because I was so nervous about Senior Night. Once we got to the Ball, I wobbled all over the place, unable to stand up straight on the dance floor. Drunk, I expressed my sexual interest to my date. He asked, "Is that the only reason you brought me here?" A girlfriend came to our table, seeing me inebriated, and helped me to the restroom. Afterward, my date refused to drive me home, so I struck him in the face. He was even more disappointed in me then. I'll never forget the look he gave me at that moment. Another friend volunteered to bring me home. I cried the entire way home, my head on the dashboard of his coveted black Lexus. Then more humiliation ensued.

The next Monday at school, the story was old news to everyone by lunch. Mrs. Thomas, our guidance counselor, questioned me about the night before. The rest of the teachers were now on guard to keep a watchful eye of me. They knew something was going on with me, "not like her," they said, like the previous semester. They approached me throughout the day at school. Each had their own different sets of serious questions and concerns. It felt good to know they cared so much, but it also felt invasive and was quite public. Worse, it made me more of a spectacle. Compared to my depression, I felt terrific. But I wasn't okay. And it wasn't safe.

I was drinking more and more often now, and starting to pursue strange men. Another alumni friend, Grace, happened to be very close with Mrs. Thomas. Grace wasn't aware anything was wrong yet. We had plans, during Mardi Gras, to eat sushi and go out. At the restaurant, I drank too much Sake and made incredible demands to the waiter. Grace became disgruntled and confused. I was speaking way too fast. I couldn't slow down -- I was speeding. After dinner, we went to a nightclub. I met a sexy Australian man who played basketball for the local college. Drunk as I was, I brought him back to Grace's with me. Luckily, my virginity scared him off. I had no idea what I was doing. Grace alerted Mrs. Thomas of the night's events. That's when the interventions started.

After hearing about this incident, my mother, alerted, stashed several pregnancy tests. She brought me to a doctor immediately. He specialized in adult psychological disorders. After an hour's discussion, he asked, "How often do you feel six foot tall and bulletproof?" "Every day," I responded, in great confidence. "Meredith, you are suffering from Bipolar II Disorder. There is a chemical imbalance in your brain. This makes you prone to severe depressions and dangerous manic episodes. It is treatable with medication and other methods. The goal will be stability." Stunned, I didn't believe what I heard. Mom was in tears, head in hands. The office prescribed medication and gave me a slot for my next appointment. This marked my transition from severe depression into severe mania. Both were true, maddening hell.

In my painting class, I was so excited about my canvas. I left for school at 5 AM one day, so I could "paint the sunrise." A police officer stopped me on the way for speeding. My art teacher reported to my mother there was more paint on me than the canvas.

The teachers, my family, friends and mother all bonded in this unprecedented anxiety. This constant fear lingered. Everyone worried what unpredictable, dangerous, or scary thing I would do next. It hurt me and confused me because I didn't know -- and I could not understand -- that anything was wrong with me.

When you're manic, no one can convince you that you are sick. You don't feel sick, and your disease tells you that you are not. You feel better than you ever have and can achieve things you never imagined. Euphoria traps you, and you're riding a constant high from which you cannot come down. I was speeding in any way you turn it. My speech, my driving, my thoughts were all racing. Yet, I kept thinking to myself, *This is the most lucid I have ever been.*

I felt like I was "back." I could talk to anyone and everyone again. People said they were so glad I was feeling good again, and they made sure to tell me they cared for me. One day the Dean of Students walked by me, delivered the basic salutations, and ended it with, "We love you, Mer." This made me think somehow they understood, and it touched me. My classmates were now more open to me and interested in what I had to say. But again, I went overboard. Though I was feeling better, things got much worse. Nothing I did now, even if it was okay, was private, or acceptable, or non-crazy behavior. I wanted to crawl into a hole.

My mania kept causing me to say things that got me into trouble, putting everyone on high alert. A classmate approached me and asked, "Are you on coke?" It crushed me because I knew it's what everyone wanted to ask. The Headmaster finally told my mother I would need to stay home for a few weeks. They wanted my medication to make me better. I was furious. "I'm finally back, and now they want to keep me at home?!"

I called the Headmaster to ask her why this was happening. She was gentle, calm and so compassionate. She did the best she could to explain to a manic person the need for a quarantine. I learned from my friends at school the Headmaster, and full staff held a meeting with our senior class. This meeting became necessary because the constant concern became such a regular topic.

My classmates didn't understand what was happening to me or why I was not at school. Lucy reported to me the most frequent comment was "there's something wrong with her." This cut me to the core like nothing ever had. I could no longer deny that yes, my mother and all my teachers and friends and doctor could not all be wrong. Yes, something was definitely wrong. But I couldn't realize it in this state.

One of the aspects that made my school so unique and special was the same reason my experience was so tenuous. Our college prep education meant smaller classes. It meant more individual time with teachers and each other. Our class graduated with forty-six students. Everyone at school saw me go through this, no exceptions. Everyone had an opinion and individual concern about it. Every bit of it was under a well-defined microscope, and it was all common knowledge.

During the at-home suspension, Lucy visited me. She brought me my art supplies and school books. Lucy was sweet, and I saw this visit as our reconnection. When she hugged me, I felt her love, her empathy and her understanding. She said, "I'm so happy you're okay, and you're getting better. I love you."

This journey changed the structure of my life forever. In this experience, my learning had only begun. For the next eight years, I would endure heartbreaking, unforgettable episodes. An unending, relentless rollercoaster of depression and mania swept me up and spit me out. Each episode was different and more challenging than the last and required hospitalization more often than not. I battled with myself. I fought taking the medications. I struggled with suicidal ideations, and the tasks necessary to achieve stability. I feared I'd never have a "normal" life. And yet, here I am.

Today, life is very different. I am so grateful to have found my challenges paved the way for my strengths. They work in tandem. I've found a way of life that works for me and have been episode-free for nearly six years. I no longer fear the stigma of my disease. I want to help those who are still suffering to find stability, peace, and their own path.

Though I would not wish this experience on my worst enemy, had it not happened, I would not be me. I would not be the woman I know, love, and respect today. I may not have found myself. I would not have met and overcome my worst challenges. My greatest demise paved the way for my greatest success.

Love is Not a Harlequin Romance

by Pamela Williams Kelly, Esq.

I was a petite 4 feet 11 inches tall. My toes hardly touched the bathroom floor as he choked me. He used the strength of his 6 feet 3-inch frame to make his point. "Get rid of them," he said. These words belonged to a stranger even though I shared his last name and called him my husband for ten years. I clawed at his hands but was helpless. I closed my eyes and thought of the hearts that beat with mine. "I won't get rid of them, but I will get rid of you. Get out!" I pushed the words out from under the hand crushing my throat. He let me go and ripped the telephone from the wall, as he stormed out. I couldn't call the police. I am not sure if I would have, even if I could. He left me feeling devastated, lost and frightened.

Count 'em! Four babies! Two were already calling me mommy, and I was two months pregnant with twins. I was in my first year of law school, unemployed and had a failed marriage. At that moment, I did what any reasonable person would have done. I cried all day and night. The next day, I made a telephone call to the clinic and asked about pregnancy termination. My stomach cringed as I listened to the explicit details of the procedure. She told me I didn't have much time and asked if I wanted to schedule an appointment. I replied, "No, I need to think about it. I will call you back." But when I hung up the telephone, I knew I wouldn't. I couldn't. How did I get here?

I grew up in a small town with a population of less than a thousand people. My parents were both religious and committed to family. They raised my sisters and me in a home filled with love and a commitment to God. My father, a strong and gentle man, hardly raised his voice to my mother. I should have had a happy childhood. But a small Mississippi town was a tough place for a girl with skin as dark as mine. I endured years of bullying; harsh jokes about my skin color— "tar baby," "skillet," they teased. Even teachers joined in on the jokes. I told my parents. But there was no relief. After a summer playing in the sun, mowing the grass and working in the garden, I returned to school and the bullying. I knew I had to learn to deal with small-town ways until I could leave.

Books were my escape from the relentless teasing. At 12 years old, I would check out a dozen at a time from the library even if I had to walk a mile home to do it. It was during one of those long Mississippi summers; I discovered Harlequin Romances. In these stories, there was always a woman and a man fighting their mutual attraction to each other. They went through resistance, challenges and conflict. But the pair would always find their way to each other and live happily ever after. Lost in the pages of these books, I learned about love. I took the pages with me the day after I graduated from high school. I was desperate to get out of the small town.

I completed my undergraduate studies, and I moved to Virginia Beach to begin a new life. While shopping in my new hometown, a handsome Navy man approached me. He was smart, romantic, attentive, and generous. He left a bouquet of roses at my door. He delivered groceries to my apartment when he saw my refrigerator was empty. He was my very own Harlequin Romance man. And I was the hapless female waiting for him to rescue me. With his next duty station set for overseas, I was excited that he would show me the world. Far from Mississippi, my destiny now seemed to be playing out like a romance novel!

My perfect world with this perfect man ended in less than six months. But it would take me another 9 ½ years of marriage before I would have the courage to end the relationship. Abuse was a story I knew well. From the bullies in school to the bigger, more relentless bully I married--each reminded me where I stood. Each attempted to convince me of their definitions of who I was in this world. I felt ashamed.

This time, I could not get lost in romance novels. I had too many responsibilities. Childhood fantasies and the need to escape a town too small for my ambition led me to this place. After ten years of disrespect, criticism, and infidelity it was time to let go of the fantasy and face reality.

My husband was on the telephone talking to his girlfriend. He hadn't been home for two days, and our 6-year-old son yearned for his father's attention. Frustrated that his "girlfriend" would hear our son, he yelled at him to be quiet and shoved him away. As I turned the corner, I watched my child crash into a large potted plant. Forgetting I had two babies in my belly to protect, I leaped at him. I kicked, smacked and punched him. I cursed him for years of humiliation, hurt and isolation. This was the last fight I would have with him. My children needed me to show up for them in a way I had not before. I decided to reclaim my identity. I was finally ready to denounce the person others wanted me to believe myself to be. To shed the false story and create my new empowered reality, I had to become my own rescuer. I let go of the damsel in distress and became the woman who didn't need romance novels to find her true happy ending.

Forgiveness When It Seems Impossible

by Nikkya Hargrove

Plastered on the red brick building, in cold, silver lettering were the words "Family Court." I never had a reason to enter into Family Court until my mother's actions brought me there. On that day we confronted our new normal as mother and daughter. We created a new definition of family. At 25 years old, I would become the mother of my mother's newborn child. He was my little brother, but I would come to call him my son. For this to work, I would have to forgive her for everything she did to get us here.

I was the only child of my parents' teenage love affair. I was three months premature. My translucent skin revealed a weak body with a strong heart. I had a determined soul, and I needed it. The first few months were touch and go. My parents were unsure if I would survive. They spiraled deeper into lives that suited them more than parenthood could. My father left for the military, and my mother used drugs.

As I stood in front of the family court judge, I was angry at my mother for all the years she failed us. Just four weeks ago she had given birth to my youngest sibling. She walked into the courtroom in her red puffy winter jacket, smelling of cigarettes. I stood in a dark blue pea coat. We made our way through the metal detectors and presumptuous stares of the guards. We sat in plastic chairs which gave no support for our backs or our emotions. It was her addiction to crack-cocaine that brought me here. I was begging to save my half-brother from foster care.

"You know Nikkya, I want my baby. I will do what I need to get him back," she told me. I believed she wanted to change, to be the mother to her son she wasn't to me. And, I wanted that as well. But there was so much she would have to do to cure this disease. I felt angry and sorry for her at the same time. The judge, a blonde haired middle-aged woman, asked me a question. "Do you commit to caring for your half-brother and providing a safe environment for him?" My answer was simple, "Yes." My mother cried. Her dark brown hair fell against my cheek as I hugged her. The love and affection I wanted to show her intertwined with anger. Her failures exhausted me.

"Yes," I will be a better mother than my mother taught me to be. I will be someone my brother can learn from and depend on. I will continue to be a daughter of which my mother can be proud.

The judge never asked questions about these. They were the things I committed to myself and this precious baby boy that day. The time I spent worrying about the well-being of my mother, her safety and livelihood now belonged to him. The baby would come first. Like that, life as I knew it changed. No more medical school to become an obstetrician. No more fiancée, she could not handle the baggage I brought with me to our relationship. I could not walk away from my brother, a newborn who needed a mother and a place to call home. I graduated from Bard College. I earned a bachelor's degree in Human Rights. Then I left a job as an Adolescent Mental Health Case Manager. I wanted to give all my being to the dysfunctional family member of mine—my mother. Gone were the days of my getting to figure out life, fresh out of college and ready to take on the world. My world now revolved around keeping myself and my brother afloat, in spite of the failures of my mother.

Gazing into his innocent eyes, I knew I was making the right decision. I told myself I was forgiving my mother for his benefit. In reality, I needed as much for me – if not more.

It was hard to remember a time when I had not been mad at her. And then it occurred to me. She had given me a gift so many longed for from their parents. I came out to her as a lesbian when I was 16 years old as if I were telling her what I ate for breakfast. We sat in the living room, lights dim, one late afternoon. I came in after school, and she happened to be there to see me, at my aunt's house. I blurted it out, in a careless, thoughtless way. "Mom, I have something to tell you. You probably already know. Or maybe you don't. But, I am gay. I like girls." Her mouth dropped. Then, she smiled, and said, "I love you. I am glad you told me. I already knew." I added her last statement to the long list of lies she'd told me already. You don't know, I said under my breath, in the way only a teenager could. I felt comfortable telling my mother. My attraction to girls, at the time, didn't carry the same weight as her drug addiction and her crimes. My sexuality was not as "bad" as her cocaine addiction, I was not killing myself. I also felt comfortable because she knew I wasn't the black sheep of the family like her. I didn't feel the need to guard my life as a secret.

My mother sat with me and asked me questions about girls I'd liked. She showed me she cared. She wanted to know all the details, even ones I wasn't ready to share. As I look back on this conversation, I know now it was the time she gave me her undivided attention. The time I told her my secret. The time I let my walls down and sat with her, the time she gave me to talk about myself wholly. And this very lesson, this approach, is how I speak to my kids. As my son morphs into a teenager, I always carve time out for him. I want him to be himself, and I leave the door open at all times. I welcome my conversations with him.

My mom was brave enough to stand up to anyone whose words, or actions, or decisions might impact her children. I wanted to call on my mama bear as she did any time she needed to in order to defend us. I saw it as a rite of passage as a mother. I also thought I needed to give birth in order for "the bear" to present herself. But, I discovered early on my mama bear was instinctual and inside of me. I learned this during my struggles with family court. I learned this from going back and forth with my half-brother's biological father. I pulled from years of examples. I remember watching my mother stand up for her children. She defended us against our fathers. She fought for us against family members who opposed our (my) sexuality. She stood up against people who accused us of stealing from a store. Her mama bear taught me lessons about being present. My mother was physically non-existent during my childhood. When she was there; I watched her. I kept my eyes on her and watched her movements, her words, her inflections. I did this to learn about who she was. About which mannerisms she had which most resembled mine.

Still, she encouraged me to follow my dreams through her unwavering support. There wasn't one dream, thought or hope I brought to her where she said to me "I don't think you should do that" or "Have you thought about..." Maybe it was because she loved me regardless of the choices I made. Maybe it was because I was the one who made the "right" decisions when compared to her many mistakes. Whatever her reasons for supporting me, I will never know. What I do know is she never dimmed any dream I had. Today, in parenting my kids, I say to them, "Have you thought about..." or "Have you noticed you're really good at..." I want them to know I support them. I also want them to know they need to be both logical and relentless when it comes to conquering their own dreams.

To forgive was to stop feeling resentful for the mistakes my mother made. I realize today that is a process. It was easier to say, "I forgive you" than it was to stop the anger. It took time, patience and reassurance she would not make the same mistake again. At 41 years old, my mother died in a half-way house. She died keeping her promise to stay on the road to recovery and did so outside of prison. When she died, my half-brother was four months old. She died from clogged arteries in her heart a disease called atherosclerosis. She was in and out of prison from the time I was born until my twenty-fourth birthday.

I'd met her before. We visited in the cold rooms of our county jail and New York State Correctional Facilities. I was thirteen. I'd met her within the confines of sterile hospital rooms after giving birth to one of my three siblings. Or on a dead-end street of Eastern Long Island after answering a call she made asking me to come and visit her. I met her at the most vulnerable periods of her life. Times in her life when she needed me. Times in her life when I could be the one to help save her from herself. Times when she yearned for me to forgive her, but my anger kept me from doing so. No matter how much I loved her in spite of her faults, I never forgot her mistakes. I became the one to pick up the broken pieces of her life. She revealed her true self to me. She did this in the weeks which followed my half-brother's birth and the weeks leading up to my mother's death. She told me things, lies she'd once told me, in her final days, she told me the truth, "Nik, I forged a check from Aunt Jo." And she confessed her feelings about the loves she had in her life, "Nik, I loved that man (Bruce)." Forgiveness of mother meant forgiving her lies and forgiving her truths. My road towards forgiveness of her began long after her death.

Forgiveness for me, in many ways, is like my mother's addiction to crack cocaine. When I am "well" I forgive her for all her mistakes, no matter how many lives she affected. I let the memories of her presence wash over me and on the good days, it's as if she is right here sitting with me. On the good days, I know deep down in my bones she is sorry for how she hurt her children. I wallow in the memories of her. I cling to the words she spoke to me from her heart and the laugh she had. I cherish the children she gave this world as her legacies. I forgive her. I know if I don't, I could not take on the responsibility of raising my son (her biological son). She gave me my first opportunity to be a mother. I don't harbor anger towards her. I could not be the mother I am today without her.

Today he throws himself into his school work with a thirst for learning about Greek mythology. He enjoys participating in local music and art programs. Through them, he can learn about commitment, determination and exploration. He is the big brother of twin sisters who are two years old. My wife and I have created a strong, stable, and loving home for our children. We raise them with a solid foundation of guidance, trust, and acceptance. We are a "take me as I am" kind of family. We have given our son (and our daughters) a life they can be proud of for which we have worked hard. A life they can stand tall in knowing they are forever loved and wanted. We talk about his "angel mommy" as we call his biological mother. He asks me questions, and I give him answers. We have open communication about his birth story. We discuss his biological parents and his adoption story— the one in which my wife and I became his legal parents. Though it's been a difficult road for us to get to where we are today as a family, we are grateful. We have faced many battles, climbed some tough hills and won. We've won the right and privilege to love one another. We do this in spite of our faults. It's because of this we live our lives in truth.

Becoming a Voice

by Pat Morgan

Maybe it was the flirting that delayed me from my biggest dream. I like to think I had other things to do before my greatest achievement in life became a reality. I went to D.C. my senior year in high school, and I was too busy flirting with some boys from North Carolina to pay attention. We went through the national archives three times, and I missed seeing the Declaration of Independence. After that trip, I always thought, "What if?"

As a young girl of 17, I missed the point in Washington the first time I went. I had a dream to dream, but it was never something I thought would actually happen. I put the idea of making a difference in D.C. on a shelf in the recesses of my mind. And so I went about doing what we do, I lived my life.

I only got to go to college for one year. My father, a deputy sheriff, was killed in the line of duty that summer and my scholarship had only been for that first year. Instead, I got married and had children and built a career in banking. I got a divorce and went into real estate and then into politics. I got married and divorced again. At 42, I was doing what I thought I needed to do. It was not a part of my narrative's landscape because it wasn't something I thought was possible. But God was busy making other plans.

I found myself volunteering at my church when it began using volunteers to help "the street people." As I walked into the great hall, I saw 10-12 of the sickest people I had ever seen in my life. I could see in their eyes and through the shuffle of their gait they believed they were lost causes. I knew many people in the world agreed. In "Mr. Smith goes to Washington," the academy award winning movie from 1939, Jimmy Stewart gave a famous speech. He said lost causes are the only causes worth fighting for and there was a reason to fight for them. I agreed. We are all called upon to "love our neighbors as ourselves." I knew the world needed more of that. When I left the church that day, I wanted to know why these people were so lost. What could I do to help them in a monumental way?

I walked in with no idea my life and my story would forever change. Homeless people became my future. I started working to understand and improve the system. And what a broken system it was. It seemed the harder I worked the more problems I found.

Why was the body count of the homeless rising? Why was it so difficult to get funding to help these people? I trudged along trying to effect change with one door after another closing in my face. I was fighting an uphill battle. I wanted to make a dent in helping these lost souls in the great hall of my church. But the bureaucracy was putting a dent in me.

The city needed funding, but they couldn't get it from the state. The state required funding but couldn't get it from the federal government. Everybody pointed the finger at someone else. I kept working to help homeless people even though I was banging my head against the wall.

Street people are not just living on the street because they choose to. Most of them are dealing with mental illness or addiction, or both. Lack of job training or greater education can add to their challenges. These factors often keep them from getting or staying employed. Some of our most vulnerable human beings are entirely left behind to try to deal with a litany of losses. Their health often declines. Loss of family and friends who might have been able to help compounds the issue. Worst of all, they've lost the mental and physical ability to "fix" it on their own. Far too often, whatever help they seek isn't there or isn't helpful. Even worse, far too many who are mentally ill are so sick they don't know they're sick. And far too many alcoholics and addicts are so ill they've given up hope of ever getting well.

In their most significant moment of need, society discards them and leaves them out in the cold. I could not stand it. The world seemed to have forgotten them. I would not.

One morning in church someone started reading from Ecclesiastes 3. "There is a time for everything, and a season for every activity under the heavens: a time to search and a time to give up, a time to keep and a time to throw away, a time to tear and a time to mend, a time to be silent and a time to speak." This got my attention. I was restless and needed to do something bigger. It was time.

In my life, I had enjoyed a successful career in banking and real estate. I had learned a lot about politics and local government as a candidate and elected official. Yet in spite of my credentials, I knew I needed to go back to college. How else was I going to figure out a way to make an impact on those who needed it the most? I took classes with people the same ages as my three sons. As I pursued my degree, I worked tirelessly to give a voice to the voiceless. Every test and every paper put me one step closer to graduating. I made sure I gave everything I had to my studies. I knew my friends on the street were counting on me to help make a difference in their lives.

My junior year in college I received a surprise from TIME Magazine. They gave me their "Rising Star" award and named me one of 20 outstanding college juniors in America. I may have been 50 years old and over the hill, but I was on a roll. That award opened the doors to American University. It also led me to then-Senator Al Gore's office where I served as an intern during my last semester. I'd campaigned for him during a couple of election cycles. But it was Arkansas Governor Bill Clinton who gave me a chance. He inspired me to do more than I ever thought a girl from Turrell, Arkansas (population 543) could do.

After graduation, I worked at "temp" agencies in Washington. Then Governor Bill Clinton decided to run for President. I worked full-time on the campaign and Presidential Transition. I was honored when President Clinton appointed me to the staff of the U.S. Interagency

Council on Homelessness. It is the pinnacle of power in policies and programs to help homeless people.

Proverbs 19:17 reads "Whoever is generous to the poor lends to the Lord, and He will repay him for his deeds." I implore those who read this to remember God's word throughout the Bible.

Isaiah 58:10 reads "If you pour yourself out for the hungry and satisfy the desire of the afflicted, then shall your light rise in the darkness and your gloom be as the noonday."

I have witnessed incredible heartache on the streets. But my homeless friends have also blessed me in ways I cannot measure. God has already begun to repay me for my deeds by blessing me with the opportunity to be a voice for the voiceless. I hope my light has risen in the darkness of each alleyway, underpass and dumpster where I have found His people living. Your light can rise too.

Mathew 25:37-40 reads, "Then the righteous will answer him, saying, 'Lord, when did we see you hungry and feed you, or thirsty and give you drink? And when did we see you a stranger and welcome you, or naked and clothe you? And when did we see you sick or in prison and visit you?' And the King will answer them, 'Truly, I say to you, as you did it to one of the least of these my brothers, you did it to me.'"

God has given clear instructions on who should care for the hungry, the hurting, the ill, the forgotten. It is up to us. You can follow His lead and effect change.

God led me to my calling. Perhaps He can lead you to one as well. Don't just read my words on this page. Help. Don't just talk about my story. Live one of your own. Mother Teresa once said, "We think sometimes that poverty is only about being hungry, naked and homeless. The poverty of being unwanted, unloved and uncared for is the greatest poverty." So won't you join me in loving and caring for those who cannot care for themselves. In the end, it is your life that will be blessed as well as theirs.

For more information, contact the designated agency in your area, or go to www.hudexchange.info/programs/coc/.

The Power of One YES

by Debrena Jackson Gandy

My husband and I walked down the aisle of our large African-inspired wedding. It was at the chic and prestigious Seattle Design Center. We wore custom-designed outfits. The scene was complete with a "village" processional. We even had a performance by a professional African dance troupe. Only thoughts of "happily ever after" filled my mind.

The notion our marriage could ever end up on the brink of divorce was the farthest thing from my mind. Divorce might happen to other people, but never to us.

We had ten years of what most would consider a happy marriage. Then our marriage experienced a crippling breakdown. We went into a downward tailspin that caused us to nearly crash and burn. For four years, starting at year 10, we tried to save our marriage, but by year 14, both my husband and I wanted out. To us, it felt like we'd "tried everything," and the only option left was to move on with divorce proceedings.

So, what occurred between the day we got married, and the day my husband and I sat down in the office of a divorce attorney? The short answer: a lot.

In the 10th year of our marriage, it came to light my husband and I had both been cheating on each other. We were both engaged in multiple sexual affairs, over a span of several years. We were both involved in what I coined in my newest book, The Love Lies, as serial infidelity. It is challenging enough to deal with one partner cheating with one person. But both of us cheated with several different individuals.

Over the course of four years, we put forth a yeoman's effort to try and save our marriage. We went to several counselors. We met with our pastor at the time, and then a second pastor, and then a therapist. We tried talking it out again and again. We read books. We had people praying for us. We would make a few steps of progress then old "stuff" would resurface. We would regress and backslide several steps.

Many evenings, I would sit in my prayer closet crying. I was feeling frustrated, powerless, helpless and lost. How did it come to this? How did we go from exchanging sweet nothings to saying nothing, and only icy silence for hours on end? What happened?

Sitting in that closet, I realized I was the one so many others threw their rope to as a lifeline. And here I was, at the end of my own rope. The one others looked to for answers was now out of them for herself.

Any hope of restoration or reconciliation seemed like a long shot in the dark. The emotional gunk, funk, and junk that had built up between us felt like a huge and steep mountain. That mountain seemed nearly impossible to climb.

One day shortly after our initial meeting with our divorce attorney, I was doing my morning prayer and meditation.

Sitting there on my bedroom floor, frustrated and teary-eyed, I admitted to God I was at the end of my rope. I was out of strategies, techniques, and new approaches. I was exhausted and ready to throw in the towel. "What do you want me to do now?!" I asked as I cried out in both anger and exasperation to God.

God's simple reply to me was: Thanks for finally asking.

It was then God presented me with an invitation.

He invited me to follow Him through a special process. Though He didn't reveal the details, He assured me my marriage was going to be better than ever. It was going to be the manifestation of the extraordinary marriage I had journaled about in my high school diary-with-the-locket days. When He mentioned what I'd written in that diary 25 years earlier, I almost fell over with surprise. I had long forgotten what I'd written, but apparently, God had not.

Before saying yes to His invitation, He let me know there was a catch. I wasn't to stray from the process or cut any corners. He would direct my every step, but I had to follow His guidance and instruction without deviation. He assured me as a result of my obedience, He would give powerful insights. These insights would enable me to be a catalyst in birthing a new paradigm for love relationships. They would allow me to transform and save marriages from any downward spirals.

Even after all this, I still hesitated. I thought to myself: What is going to be so new or different that I haven't already tried? What if it didn't work? What if we invested a lot of time and energy only for me to be right back where I started, at square one? After four years of working hard to try and save our marriage, I was both skeptical and resigned. Most of all, I was emotionally worn out. I asked God, "Are you sure this is going to help a lot of other people?"

God's answer was an unequivocal "Yes."

So, in that pivotal moment, I let out a big sigh and decided my answer would be "yes" to this invitation. At that moment, the destiny of my marriage acquired a new trajectory. This yes was to change me, my marriage, and my life—forever. It was a decision that was to become a critical turning point.

Over the next 90 days, I received a series of what I can best describe as "divine downloads." They came through me, not from me. Every other day I received another download. I penned the term "Love Lies," and I identified 50 along gender lines: 25 specific to women and 25 specific to men. They blew my mind.

Along the way, I discovered "Love Lies" were present in every aspect of my relationships. They were in my thoughts, actions, emotions and behaviors. This was a tough pill to swallow. My ego shouted, "no not me!"

At that time, I had two best-selling books under my belt. For nearly 15 years, I'd been designing and leading personal growth and spiritual development events and courses. I considered myself rather evolved.

As I recognized each Love Lie, I was able also to identify how and where it began. This enabled me to pull it out by the root. The process started with me and then rippled outward to my husband and then our marriage.

My personal healing became the catalyst for the transformation of my marriage. Over the next two years, our relationship completely turned around.

The first year I followed the instructions and the "divine coaching" given to me by the Holy Spirit. I didn't tell my husband. I didn't announce it to my friends; I did the "divine self-work" I was being instructed to do. Day by day, and week by week.

It was a faith walk because the Holy Spirit was only illuminating one or two steps in front of me at a time. Each month had a different focus. I noticed that as I started to transform, my husband's response to me began to change. The way we related and engaged with each other started to transform too. And thus, my marriage began to transform.

I recall the month where God spoke to me about what it means to submit to your husband. It was vastly different from anything I'd ever heard in any Bible study or sermon.

To say to a wife, you have to submit to your husband were fighting words. Why was this? Because, as God showed me, I didn't understand the true meaning of submitting. In relation to covenant marriage and God's Divine Design of marriage, He began to show me a new meaning.

In the context of covenant marriage, the husband and wife have different Divine Assignments. These assignments are aligned with the unique character of man and woman. As God reminded me, roles are not scriptural. The term is not used in the Bible where the Divine Assignments of husband and wife are laid out. Furthermore, roles are limiting, the Holy Spirit explained. And marriage, as God designed it, is enables us to be more free in our spirit, not less free.

For example, in the context of marriage, to submit means one of two things, depending on the situation. It means to yield or allow. When I asked God to give me an example, He brought to mind my driver education classes from high school. These classes taught us what it meant to yield. As you entered the flow of traffic, you were to adjust your speed and yield to the oncoming traffic. This would help to keep the flow of the existing traffic and prevent an accident. Interestingly enough, we've digressed to expecting the oncoming traffic to yield to us instead of us yielding to it. God explained it is very similar in marriage. The wife is to yield to her husband's suggestions, ideas, or perspective. She is to allow him to help, aid, or contribute to her. Allowing also means to let his love in, and to allow your love to flow to him, unimpeded.

One of many other revelations I had during that time was about respect. In Ephesians, the assignments of husband and wife are clearly laid out. A wife is to respect her husband. Interestingly, this is an assignment specific to the wife. It is not part of the husband's responsibilities. He has a different set of assignments. In the context of covenant marriage, respect has a very different meaning from the definition you might find in Webster's dictionary.

God instructed me to "break down" the word respect into its Latin roots. "Re" means again, and "-spect" means to see, as in the root of the words spectator, spectacle, or spectacles (like glasses). So, one of the wife's assignments is to be able to SEE her husband with fresh eyes, again and again. Daily. She is to SEE him without holding grudges. See him without closing her heart to him. See him without giving him the Silent Treatment. See him without harboring negative emotions or suppressing anger. This is a tall order for a wife. This was a tall order for me. This meant that I had to see my husband, NOT as his behavior, but with the eyes of my heart. I needed to see him with a heart that was in a constant process of releasing and forgiving.

I had never, in all my years of attending various churches, EVER had respect explained to me like this! No wonder Christian marriages have the same high failure rate of non-Christian marriages in the U. S.—51%!!!! By the way, we have the highest marriage failure rate in the world!!

I first started sharing a few of these downloads in 2009 during a monthly teleseminar. It attracted men & women from all over the country. This soon evolved into a LIVE seminar in my living room with eight friends. And that progressed into the birth of a live full-day course called the "Love Academy."

Since that first event in my living room, the Love Academy has changed the lives of hundreds of participants across the country. We eventually expanded to include live for-men-only "Men-tality" seminars. The Love Academy and Men-tality Courses gave rise to my newest book, The Love Lies.

I am humbled and amazed at all God has done through my own struggles and surrender. It was all the result of my Yes. To date, I'm aware of at least 31 new marriages that have resulted from graduates of the Love Academy. It is amazing!

I think back to that fateful day in my prayer closet when God first posed that invitation to me. I am so thankful I said YES. It led me to stand in the gap for others. Because of everything I went through I am able to help others on their journey. Little did I know where that YES would lead me.

Trust the Process

by Siobhan Renee Riley

I sat in my sixth-grade class wearing my favorite dress—the white one with the beautiful blue bow on the side. When my teacher called me to the front of the room and told me to bring all my belongings, I knew something was wrong. A school administrator took me by the hand and walked me down the hall to a room everyone in the school recognized. There were two students already seated. I introduced myself, as instructed. Afterward, I unpacked my books and took a seat in one of a dozen empty seats. I would spend the rest of the school year in this class for students who were not as advanced as the others.

Tests said I was reading at a third-grade level. I could read the words. But somewhere between the spaces and lines, the words lost their meaning. I couldn't understand what I was reading. But I understood humiliation.

That evening, I ran home faster than I ever had before. I went straight to my room and cried. I didn't understand why I couldn't learn like the normal students. I felt stupid. I felt like something was broken in my head, and nothing would fix it.

That day was not the end of the humiliation I suffered. My academic struggles would continue through middle school. Year after year, I was reminded I was not smart enough. The frustration was often more than I could handle. I was very insecure in spite of all my family's efforts to encourage me.

After dinner, my mom and I would read books together. Once we completed one, I would write a book report for her. It wasn't long before I started creating my own stories. I would sit in my bedroom for hours writing about children who saved the world. The characters were all kids like me. They learned a little differently from other children. They became leaders who brought world peace. One kid, a sixth-grader who read on a third-grade level, even became a journalist and TV personality. That kid was me.

Over the years, I grew from difficulties comprehending to being able to think on my feet. When I sat in that room with my 6th-grade teacher, I realized my perspective was off. It wasn't that I wasn't smart. I needed to change my way of thinking. I needed to keep telling myself I could overcome one of my biggest challenges. The more I told myself that, the more I started to believe it.

By the time I completed middle school, I finally started to feel somewhat more confident. When I got to the 9th grade, my English teacher told my mother I had the highest grade in the class. High school was a turning point for me, and English became my favorite subject. I realized reading comprehension wasn't as hard as I once thought. I found creative writing classes intriguing. I attributed my new perspective to my teacher's belief in me, which led to me believing in myself.

Many of my teachers doubted I could overcome my learning difference. But there was one who encouraged me in my writing. One day he had an announcement for the class. I got butterflies in my stomach when he told them I had one of the highest scores on the state writing test.

I started writing so much, poetry became my saving grace. I competed in the Miss Teen of the Triad Pageant my junior year in high school while reciting a poem I wrote. I was 2nd runner-up. College boosted my confidence considerably. I graduated Summa Cum Laude with a major in journalism and mass communication. My first day at CBS News as a college intern in New York was a dream come true. I couldn't believe a person who struggled as much as I did could become a reporter and anchor. But it happened after graduation. It was as my 10th-grade teacher predicted. Whenever I started to second guess myself, I remembered his words, "This name I'm about to call is someone who is smart. She's going places. She's going to be successful. We're going to see her on the big screen one day."

Television news had its ups and downs. One moment, in particular, I find hard to forget. It happened during a primetime news report about Michigan traffic. I had inadvertently drawn an image resembling a penis on a smart board. The segment was live, and video of the drawing went viral. The humiliation was as intense for me that evening as it had been the day 25 years before. Fellow journalists were mocking me. It was just like when the kids in the advanced class had made fun of my placement in the remedial program. And as I had years before, I went home and cried. This time, I didn't cry because I wasn't smart enough. I cried because it seemed no matter what I accomplished humiliation was a part of my process.

I dried my tears and worked through the embarrassment. I decided not to focus on negativity. Yes, I would make mistakes. Yes, things would happen that might be a little embarrassing. But humiliation occurs when others make you feel low or reduced somehow. Being moved to a remedial class made me feel less than a student. For a brief moment, the mocking of the internet over the television gaffe made me feel less than a journalist. That day, I wrote a letter to the sixth grader who still lives in me. I let her know she is smart, she is clever, and she is far more powerful than she'll ever know. I told her she would not be able to stop the derailments, difficulties, challenges or mistakes. Those things would be a part of her process. But she would not let them reduce her.

After ten years as a very successful TV journalist, I went on to become a marketing and media executive. Every day, I face difficult topics. I have to make tough decisions and deal with people who behave like sixth graders. I accept it as part of the process. But I haven't quit. I'll never quit. I've grown to appreciate the people who want their negative words to shrink my hopes and dreams. Every obstacle I faced taught me trials don't come to destroy anyone. Trials are to strengthen us.

When God was taking me to the next level, things were sometimes uncomfortable. It was hard to see the light at the end of the tunnel, but I never lost my faith. My faith carried me through some of my darkest moments. It wasn't easy to keep going, but I always reminded myself God would never leave me nor forsake me. That has made all the difference!

Give Up or Get Up

by Reverend Marilynn Robinson

I grew up in the projects in the Bronx, in New York City, with parents who had limited education. I often had to figure things out on my own. In any situation, we have a choice... to give up or to get up. I had to get up in my spirit to pursue my dream job.

I discovered my career path through summer jobs I took while in college. These jobs gave me exposure to hospital administrators. Something about the job stuck with me. Once I figured out which career I wanted, I had an incredible sense of direction.

I knew which classes I needed to take to get into graduate school. I took the classes. I wanted to go to the Yale School of Public Health. I knew I had to do well on my exam to get accepted. I did well and went to my dream school. One by one, I checked off each requirement on my list.

When I moved to Nashville, I found a position I thought would be challenging and could benefit me. As I began to prepare for my interview, I thought back to all my work in the hospitals across the northeast. And yet with all my experience, I knew I had not run a medical practice. I wanted this job. My husband and I had twin daughters who were two years old at the time. We agreed when we moved to Nashville, he would go to Divinity School full-time. He'd need to cut back to part-time work in his physician practice to do this, so we needed my salary. My family's financial security depended on it.

During my interview, I could tell the doctors and nurses were not impressed. I assumed it was due to my lack of experience in this field. They were looking for someone who had done this before. While on break, I said a silent prayer asking for guidance on how to turn this interview around. I knew who I was and what I had to offer. I had an excellent education and great experience. But I had no prior experience in the specific job they were trying to fill. Yet, God reminded me this was not different from anything I had ever done. I had to get up in my perspective of myself and what I had to offer to this job. Yes, the interview was not going well, but it wasn't over. I had time to redeem myself.

I went back for the conclusion of the interview, armed with my newfound confidence. The Chairman of the Family Practice was waiting. I said, "If you're looking for someone with experience running a physician practice, I'm not your person. But if you're looking for someone innovative, resourceful, energetic, committed and ready to implement best practices, then I'm the person you want!" I got the job.

Bottom line... it makes sense to be transparent. I didn't have the experience. No sense pretending I did have it. Too often we, as women, think it makes us look weak when we are transparent and honest about who we are. In reality, we do best to acknowledge our weaknesses and mistakes and turn them around to our advantage.

After my first year in graduate school, I interviewed for a prestigious summer fellowship. I walked into the room where the other students were waiting. They all had on black suits—men and women. I had on a red and white dress with elephants all over it. "I didn't get the memo to wear a black suit," I said as I entered the interview, "but I'll know what to wear from now on." My parents weren't well educated. They didn't know to teach me what to wear for an interview. I had to learn by observing others. It made no sense to me to act like I didn't realize I was not dressed appropriately for this interview. I owned it.

During the interview, I spoke about my qualifications, accomplishments, and persevering attitude. I told them about my recognition as the top student at the Yale School of Public Health. I got the fellowship. The woman who interviewed me became one of my most important mentors in the business world.

I learned not to be afraid or embarrassed about what you don't know. Look at your strengths and focus on them. Acknowledge your shortcomings. Don't be defensive. Be real and humble. Laugh at yourself. If you say it first, others have no power over you when they comment on it. I have found people appreciate those characteristics. If you allow them, folks will help you achieve your goals. Transparency, honesty, a sense of humor and a willingness to change go a long way. It will take you all the way to success!

Sewing a Broken Heart

by Kathryn Vigness

I remember it like it was yesterday. I was 15 years old and in love with my high school sweetheart. It was a cloudy, overcast day in late March. I will never forget the sound of the 1983 tan Chevy thundering down the gravel road. I could feel the floorboards shaking under my feet. The smell of spring right around the corner as the last of the snow had melted, and water filled the ditches. With a sweet smile and a heavy heart, I reached over and slid my hand into his. Somehow, I knew we wouldn't be together forever.

"Watch Out!" I yelled as the tires slid on the gravel road. We could hear metal crunch, glass shattering, and finally a deafening silence. When I came to, I was lying down in the middle of a field. As I stood, I was more disorientated and confused than hurt. The impact threw my body 500 yards from the 4-door Citation, yet I had no recollection of it. And then I saw him. Lifeless. I needed to save him.

I walked through fields, ditches and down a long gravel road. I found the nearest farmstead and got help. Time stood still amidst the panic. The ambulances were the first to arrive, followed by our parents. Then there was the deafening whooshing of the chopper landing to whisk me away. I could not comprehend the severity of it all, so I closed my eyes and prayed.

After the barrage of tests pokes, and prods, my prognosis was serious. I had hirteen broken bones and internal injuries. But, I could not think of myself. My mom approached. It was the first I had seen her since the accident. It was not good news. My boyfriend of two years was gone. I was the one driving. It was my fault. My bones were fractured, organs torn, and my heart shattered like the windshield of the Chevy. From inside and out, I was broken. I can still feel it, even today.

If I could tell my fifteen-year-old self one thing, it would be this: Your bones; they will heal. You have already defied the odds because you will walk again. You will carry three beautiful babies full term. You will treat your body like the temple she is. There will be many lessons you will learn on this journey of self-love and self-discovery. I promise you, bones will heal. Your heart? Girl, that'll take some work.

It wasn't my first heartbreak. I had already dealt with the tragic loss of my brother. I had lived through the pain of having doctors diagnose my mom with a brain tumor. Now there was a new broken piece amidst the others.

When a heart shatters, putting it back together is like completing a jigsaw puzzle. Some days nothing seems to fit, and other days the pieces meet perfectly. And one day, after many, many years, I came to a cruel realization. I didn't have all the pieces to the puzzle. I would use what I had left and pick up more pieces along the way through love, healing, and giving. New pieces. Different fabrics. Woven. Patched.

Cemented in. I sewed unconventional fragments that didn't quite fit but filled the nooks and crannies.

First was my gratitude journal, the one I received while still in the hospital. In it, I recalled everyday life moments. Finding the silver lining even in the ugliest situation cemented a new foundation in my life. In time, I discovered extraordinary in the mundane. And seventeen years later, faith and optimism for a brighter day still carry me. For as much I tried to avoid it, I did find love again. Love, partnership, and commitment would intertwine to create something new.

I asked the universe to send me boys who would never leave me. The universe answered with the births of my three sons. And like that, mother's love was the next texture woven through my heart. Each of my children were like a piece of the canvas creating a newer, stronger heart for me. The building of my heart as a mother was not without its challenges. I lived in a fog of postpartum depression for the first three years of motherhood. Failed nursing, colic and depression plagued our initial bonds. Yet my heart stretched and expanded in more ways than I can imagine. Witnessing their first smile gave me strength. The smell of a fresh bath, their unending giggles, and hearing them say "I love you" all became patches to my heart. James stitched in awareness. Jack sewed in vision, and my dear Drew was the layer of healing that fortified it all.

Even a decade later, I lived with the heaviness, an intense aching I accepted as a part of me. My journey of self-love and healing required much affirmation. "I see you. I forgive you. I love you. I let you go to create a new story." This mantra chanted in my head until my heart could extend the grace I needed to forgive myself. With affirmations like these, I spoke to the 15-year-old and released her pain. I gave her permission to renew. Transformed from a broken girl to the woman I had become. Letting go of the harsh judgments and self-blame set me free once and for all.

Finally, I let light fill the depths of my heart. I trusted my soul and flew, alone, across the world to Bali to climb Mount Batur, an active volcano. I put a sacred temple on my vision board where it remained for a full year. One day as I was looking for yoga teacher training, an opportunity in Bali showed up. I looked over at my vision board, and the same photo I had posted was on the screen of my laptop. I was ready to go. The hike started at 4 am. It was so dark. You could only see one step ahead. Climbing the mountain was symbolic of the all the challenges I have faced. It was a reminder to honor every step I take and to focus on a single step at a time. At 6 am, I watched the sun rise above the water and mountains. I released the last remaining darkness that consumed me. The sun's light-filled me with peace to know my heart was finally complete. I now trust I am precisely where I need to be, and I am who I should be.

I do not have the same heart of that 15-year-old girl. Now my heart is new, stronger and more resilient. It has seen and felt war, grown new life, opened, closed, and reopened old scars. My heart has light and love beating through every single fiber of its divine tapestry.

Be-u-tiful

by Jasmine "Jaz" Gray

I was thirsty. I was so thirsty, and the nurse wouldn't give me anything to drink. I kept thinking, *I've had so many surgeries. I can always get some Sprite, some water, ice chips or something when I wake up.*

This lady kept trying to divert my attention. The anesthesia from my 12-hour procedure had not worn off yet, so it was hard to focus. I concentrated on the light above the recovery room bed. I counted the white ceiling tiles around it. Then, I asked the nurse again. Still no drink. She walked up close to my bedside and put her hand in mine. She said, "May I pray for you?"

People I know have prayed for me before. Medical personnel usually try to be politically correct and stay away from religion. Immediately, my stomach did a flip-flop. I thought, God, what's going on? I did a half-nod in her direction. She put her other hand on my forehead and closed her eyes. I closed mine.

When I awoke the second time, they had moved me from recovery to a single-unit hospital room. They had dimmed the lights and closed the curtains, but I could still make out my mother. She was giving me this strange look. In the 22 surgeries I had up to that point for my rare birth defect— arteriovenous malformation (AVM)--I had never received a look like that one. And in the 20 still to come, I would never see it again.

It was a mixture of disbelief and hurt. The look said, "Lord ... look at my baby." Something was wrong, worse than usual, and I had to know. "What?" I asked her. Momma tilted her head and started to move her hand in a circular motion over her right cheek. "All this had to be removed," she said. "It was infected. It's gone."

I didn't cry when my mother told me half of my face was missing. But as I sat in my doctor's office months later, it took all my strength not to flood the room with my tears. Dr. Suen told me I would most likely never be able to give a full smile again.

In an instant, my naivety was gone. I felt like water. It may seem cliché. People overuse water analogies, but I felt like I had melted. I was in another form now. I wanted to deal with reality, to be OK with what God was allowing to happen to me. I didn't want to lose my mind. I needed to be liquid and flexible. I couldn't have any more disappointment or unattainable fantasies about where all my surgeries would eventually lead.

I was at the crux of womanhood. I was old enough to know fairytales are just made up stories built on cultural values. Yet, I was young enough to believe in them anyway. Like other women from 9 to 99, I had an idea in my head about ideal beauty that was wholly unattainable. I pressed on anyway. With each subsequent surgery, I was more focused on what I would look like afterward. I should have focused on how I would feel.

As a foodie, it was pure torture to have surgeries followed by feeding tubes or staples placed in my tongue. I watched my parents and sister eat, while I closed my eyes and sniffed the aroma. Because of the rapidly flowing blood vessels, I would bleed all over the floor. Random spasms of pain left me breathless. There were stitches, bandages, and skin grafts. Side effects of experimental treatments. Lockjaw and the loss of my bottom mandible. These were all tough pills to swallow. I had to learn how to speak, how to eat, how to control my saliva. These were lessons I wish I hadn't needed to learn.

But none of them kept my mind racing, and my knees bent in prayer most nights. The droop under my eye, the puff of my cheek, the bulge in my jaw bone, the fat under the implant in my chin, the absence of real lips, the way missing muscles made my face pull to the side all could bring me to tears. I told myself there was such a thing as "normal," and one day I would be it. I dreamed of that day. I even made plans for it. And then month after month, change after change, I was looking more and more peculiar (disfigured by surgeries). They removed the most-concerning AVMs and my health stabilized.

One Sunday, I finally felt "acceptable" enough to show my face at church. It wasn't my church because it would have been too much. I was sitting next to my Daddy in my bandages trying to be as invisible as possible as the preacher began speaking.

I realized the sermon was about the apostle Paul. Cool, I know about Paul, I thought. Paul had a health challenge. And Paul begged God several times to take it away. God said, "no." Wait, say what now?

I squinted my eyes and took a deep breath. God told Paul he needed the weakness because it kept him humble. It made him stronger. I scrolled down in my Bible to where the minister was now quoting Jesus. I had been deep in my thoughts and lost track.

"My grace is sufficient for you because my power shows itself most effectively in your weakness," Jesus said.

My next thought was, So ... Could I look like this forever? And that's when the vanity of it all hit me. I felt something. Guilt at first, but then something else. A weight lifting? Call me a pragmatist, realistic, or just "woke." But sitting in that pew, it was life-altering to grapple with this fact. My external attractiveness was not as important to God as it was to me. It was freeing to know He would develop who I was as a person—by any means necessary.

What do you do when you realize, despite having faced real life-threatening circumstances, your emotional well-being is actually tied to aspects of your journey that don't really matter? What do you do when you realize the one thing you want most is not what's best for you? You surrender.

When I consent to my human missteps, I can see the divine path forward God has conceived. Normality is not an aim worth the energy. It's like fighting traffic on Thanksgiving to pick up Glory greens from the grocery store, waiting forever in one of the handfuls of open lines, and then finding out my grandmother has a homemade pot of collards simmering on the stove. It's like rushing past the homemade fudge samples only to pay for a prepackaged candy bar on my way out.

Eventually, I gained enough wisdom only to accept definitions of beauty that included how I look. When I decided I no longer desired normalcy, I could even define beauty for myself. I outgrew all the boxes of what other people thought I would need to do, be or look like to succeed in mainstream society.

I then moved to one of the most glamorous cities in the United States, Los Angeles. I started looking for work in the most superficial industry in the world—entertainment. I went on a dozen interviews, and every single one of them rejected me. Sometimes, it was as soon as I sat down and the interviewer took a good look at me.

But I would no longer play it safe, small and stifled. I pushed on. I interned for BET, assisting with their award shows and scripted TV shows. I worked for film festivals. I handled everything from programming to interviewing filmmakers after screenings. I worked with screenwriters, reading their scripts and providing them with feedback. Finally, a year after making my leap of faith, I landed a job. I went from unemployed to working for one of the top major film studios in the world. With God's favor, I was able to make a mark. I was cultivating connections. I began bringing in film projects. And I was attending some of the most prestigious festivals in the world as a film buyer.

Early in my career at the movie studio, I sat down with a company executive for an informational interview. He said something that has always stuck with me. He said he knew the company was a cool place to work because they hired someone as unique as me and I was thriving there.

We must remember cookie cutter will never be better than made-from-scratch. For me to become everything God has called me to be, He made every ingredient necessary. Even the blood, the sweat and the tears. Be-u-tiful. Be You. I am rising by heat and with pressure, baking to a golden brown. Since the fires of life are refining me, I've decided to embrace the process.

One Day at a Time

by Amy Speropolous

For many people, denial is a gun loaded with lies. Every day, they play a game of Russian roulette in their heads. They load up the lies and live in the denial that has become their lives. They pull the trigger day after day, while taking risk after risk. Some will cling to the denial. That leads them to a destination of hospitalization, prison or death.

Columbia University did a study on addiction and here is some of what they found. More than 40 million Americans age 12 and over meet the clinical criteria for addiction. Some of them will never seek the help they need. Others will fight through the fog of addiction and find a path to recovery.

This is one of those stories. It is my reality. It has been for a long time. You see, addiction is a family disease. It's the ones who love the addict—the children, the spouse or the parents—who often suffer the most. They don't drown away their sorrows in a bottle, so they witness everything. They are not numb to the effects and have to bear the brunt of the pain and anger.

I know this because my father was an alcoholic. It took a long time for me to see it because he was such a driven man.

He graduated on the dean's list at the University of Alabama. In the Army National Guard, he was a Green Beret where he learned to work hard, train hard and live hard. He had jobs with the Internal Revenue Service and the Drug Enforcement Agency. He was always thought of as an enforcer. He climbed the ladder in his career and captured the bad guys.

If he could do all that with a drink in his hand, there was no way he had a problem with alcohol, right? That is what we told ourselves. That is what others tell themselves every day. They protect themselves with denial. I should know. I am an alcoholic, too.

So how did it happen? How did I watch alcohol grab ahold of my father and not realize when it did the same to me?

Let me start at the beginning. I grew up in a middle-class family in Birmingham, Alabama. My parents believed in the American dream. The also ate, slept and breathed Alabama football. Mix in the fact I was born in the '70s and the peace-and-love movement hadn't wound down yet. Put all these elements together, and it was the perfect recipe and excuse for lots of drinking.

I wanted to follow in the footsteps of my dad. So I insisted on being the life of the party. I was an outspoken child who never met a stranger. From a young age, I was eager to stand by his side as he drank the night away.

We never talked about his drinking though. Like a lot of families, we swept it under the rug.

Mom said Daddy was "tired," "overworked" or "stressed out." But I knew. In fact, I tried to stop it.

I remember pouring vodka out of the bottles and filling them with water on too many occasions to list. That didn't work. The alcohol failed to numb his pain and block out his world, so he started coming around less and less.

My mother got pregnant again. She probably thought it would help stop my father's drinking and save their marriage. In the end, things got worse.

I tried so hard to fix him; to fix my parents; to save our family. But I was only eight years old. When my mother filed for divorce, I felt it was my fault.

I didn't see much of my dad after he left our home. He went on to create a new family. I became lost in my schoolwork.

My mother was strict. In fact, kids teased me in high school because I was the only one with a ridiculously early curfew. Partying was not in the plans, so I became devoted to making something better of myself.

There was never a question of where I would go to college. From the moment I was born, my parents started grooming

me for The University of Alabama. That's where I headed the minute I graduated. I planned to pursue my own American dream in broadcast journalism.

Tuscaloosa is where I started drinking for the first time. From the moment I took that first sip, I didn't stop. Alcohol took control of me. I considered it my favorite companion. It was with me through the football seasons, the parties, the studying and the pursuit of a degree. As long as my grades were good, I told myself I had a handle on it.

I drank through my college years and right into my career. I thought I had everything under control, so I brought alcohol into my marriage.

I had no trouble abstaining from alcohol when I was pregnant. All three times, I was able to focus on bringing healthy children into the world. I felt so blessed. Each time they put one of my children in my arms, I would revel in the miracle of it all. Then I would drink to celebrate as soon as I was able.

I believed I was normal. I drank to the point of blacking out on a regular basis after my kids grew older. I told myself I was "tired." I lived in denial to make it all OK. I told people, "Sure sometimes I drink too much." I didn't even try to hide it. I thought everybody drank like me.

As a journalist, my job is to tell the truth and uncover the facts. I learned to play a part and compartmentalize my life, so I could function while drinking. The real truth was my family was falling apart. My husband wanted to help me. He attempted all the tricks loved ones try. He asked me to promise to stop drinking. So I made a vow to him I would stop. As soon as I thought enough time had gone by I poured another drink. He threatened to leave, but I would convince him to stay.

Then March 5, 2014, happened. The most precious parts of my life were in my care, and I drove home drunk with my three little girls in the car. We only had six miles to go between the restaurant and our house. I passed out three times; once in the parking lot of the restaurant, again at a red light and finally in our driveway. To this day I don't know how we made it home.

I'm grateful no one died that day. I'm thankful my daughter was brave enough to do what was right and call her father to tell him I was drunk. When she had the courage to make that call, she may have saved my life. In fact, she may have saved us all.

I'm grateful my husband loved me enough to threaten to leave and take my kids. I am grateful I somehow realized I would not be able to talk him out of it. I haven't had a drink since that day.

When I started my path to recovery, it was strange. I had to learn how to live without a drink in my hand. In the end, I found the road to recovery, and I continue to walk on it every day. God loved me enough to give me grace and mercy. He restored my life to sanity!

When I was little, I wanted to be like my father. In many ways, I am. I am determined and driven. I don't give up. I love Alabama football, and I am an alcoholic.

Unlike my father, this disease did not kill me. He died at 55. His father also died from the disease. By the grace of God, I am a survivor. Now I live my life one day at a time. I paid a price for this life I live, and I don't ever want to forget that!

Which takes me back to Alabama. Bear Bryant was one of the greatest coaches who ever lived. When he coached the Alabama football team, he kept a folded piece of paper tucked into the corner of his wallet. He would often pull it out and read it to the players. They found it in his wallet when he died.

It read:

This is the beginning of a new day.

God has given me this day to use, as I will.

I can waste it or use it for good.

What I do today is very important because I am exchanging a day of my life for it.

When tomorrow comes, this day will be gone forever, leaving something in its place I have traded for it.

I want it to be gain, not loss—good, not evil.

Success, not failure in order that I shall not forget the price I paid for it.

Bear Bryant lived by these words. And now so do I, one day at a time.

Finding My Way

by Sherica Hymes

It was a good day. I woke up and felt peace in my soul and was ready for anything. I prepared myself for work, got ready for a big day and I was excited. I was a project manager working on a program that would be broadcast live to thousands of people that afternoon. I worked incredibly hard to prepare, and I was ready. I knew I was going to knock it out of the park and nothing was going to stop me. I was in complete control of my day.

We all have days like this. We wake up on top of the world ready to face whatever life throws at us. But what happens when that world falls apart in a split second? What happens when you have always been the one to hold it all together and you just can't anymore? Who helps the helpers when they break? I was about to find out.

The live broadcast was going even better than I expected. In between segments, I felt the need to check my phone for the very first time that day. Something just nudged me. So I grabbed it on my way out to get some fresh air. I saw several missed calls from a number I didn't recognize. As I was searching the recesses of my mind to figure out who it might be the phone rang again. This time I knew the number. It was a dear friend, and I answered right away. "Where are you?" she asked. I told her I was at work and I only had a minute to talk. The phone started to ring again, and the same unrecognizable number popped up on my screen. These people were persistent. Something told me I better answer. I told my friend I had another call and she said, "Don't answer it. I have to tell you something. Are you sitting down?" But my heart told me to take the call, so I did. I told her to hold on, and I clicked over.

"Hello?"

"Is this Sherica Hymes?"

"Yes"

"This is the Memphis Police Department and..." at that moment my heart started to beat faster. Much faster.

"Where are you? We need to come meet you?"

I couldn't comprehend what was going on. My entire world was spinning out of control. As the police officer started to explain what was going on, I caught bits and pieces of what he was saying. Each word was like a dagger in my heart. "Your son...." "Missing....." "Posted video....." "Saying goodbye......"

I felt my chest getting tight. My eyes couldn't focus. I wanted to close my eyes and wake up from this nightmare playing out on the other end of the phone. I wanted him to stop talking. I somehow mustered the words, "I'll meet you at my house."

My son had been through a lot in the days leading up to this. He had suffered major losses in every area of his life. He had slipped into a really dark place. The losses had taken their toll- And now nobody could find him.

I clicked back over to my friend, and she gave me some more details. My family had known for a little while about his videos and they were out looking for him. They were trying to find him for me. I rushed home to meet the police officers. After giving them some background information and a clear description, they issued a city-wide missing-person report and gave me explicit instructions regarding next steps. As soon as they were gone, I left with my Dad to find my son.

We found out he contacted a friend and was planning to meet him. We needed to intercept, to get to him fast and first. We rushed to the meeting location at a gas station and found him there. It became chaos. He was suffering, scared and exhausted. He was not aware that the police had put out a missing person report on him. He was confused to see them there. People stopped to look, many of them attempting to make this a "viral" moment at my family's expense, while time stood still for my son and me. He just wanted it to end. I was terrified something bad was going to happen. One wrong move on either parties' part could be disastrous.

The Crisis Intervention Officer in charge gave instructions to his peers to manage the crowd. He and I focused on my Son.

I felt like the bottom was falling out and I wasn't sure I would be able to calm him. I also realized control of the situation didn't belong to me. That is a tough realization for someone who was always in control. It's even tougher when your child's life is on the line.

My control issues had been a constant companion my entire adult life. At the young age of 15, I was raped by a friend's uncle. Once the act itself was over, I went home and immediately showered. I took a hot bath and stayed in it until the water got cold. Then I did them both all over again just to be sure. I convinced myself if I could get clean quickly enough I could act like it never happened. I swore that was the last time I would be in a situation where I wasn't in control. And that is what I fought to do.

That battle had had an immeasurable impact on my career, my relationships, my finances and my health. At work, I fought to get noticed. I didn't want to give up any power to my peers. So I tried to work harder than everybody else. If that didn't work, I would leave and go somewhere else where I could maintain control. I was a serial dater with a list of requirements for how each person was supposed to treat me. Again, I wanted to be in control. I would try to budget and be responsible, but even that felt like I wasn't in control. I wanted to do what I wanted to do. Then the health issues started. I had five major surgeries in four years. The last one with odds that I may not survive at all. All the while I was still convinced I was keeping it all together.

Standing in the parking lot of that gas station I watched my son. I wanted to take away his pain, but I knew I couldn't. I no longer wanted to be in control. I had to surrender. The world needed to understand I was not ok. I just wanted him to be ok. It took some time, but we were able to calm him down. We were able to get him the rest and care he needed.

To make it through the tough times, I had to make my circle smaller. I had to give myself time to process everything. Some days I just sat on my couch and stared at the walls while I rocked back and forth. I did what I needed to do to make it through. I stopped trying to take care of everything. I let go. I acknowledged that I needed help. I denounced Super Woman and realized the "Cape" was not real—gladly.

My son is on the road to recovery. He is back in school and doing well. He is learning how to make his circle smaller and to ask for help. He continues to work hard every day to understand how to live healthy and take care of himself. He is teaching me to do the same. I am amazed at his resilience. My recovery from control is ongoing as well.

There are many days when I slip back into the need to fix things to control them. I still try to play the role of the caretaker at times. But I am much stronger and wiser because I have been through these struggles. In the end, I had to lose control in order to find my way.

Learning to Live

by Amy Lorton

All my life I've been a geek. In the world of not fitting in, social disasters and mortifying shyness, I ruled. Yep, that was me: Sheena, Queen of the Bungle. But many years ago, I began to change. And today, I have a number of good friends, many who think I'm quite normal. I also don't hesitate to go to a party filled with strangers or even talk to someone new. I have begun to live. And it all was because of someone who did not.

I lost my best friend after four years of illness. It was unexpected, although I knew it was a "someday" thing. Her last years were filled with more diagnoses than you could shake a thermometer at and countless trips to many doctors. In the end, none were much help. She suffered a lot of physical and emotional pain. But through the heartache for her family and me, a miracle happened.

I used to be a socially inept, overweight loner. My only friends were characters you could find on television and in novels. Seven years ago I met my rescuer. She was an extremely beautiful, gregarious person who couldn't stand to see anyone not having fun.

I had nothing in common with this person. She had more dates and social events lined up than a Kardashian on a Saturday night. But she wouldn't take "no" for an answer.

Country club dance? "You have to go," she said. I declined many of her invitations to lighten me up. Yet her answer was always the same: "Be ready because I'm coming to get you."

Finally, she wore me down. And for the first time in years, life became fun again. It was filled with trips to the beach, Tae-Bo workouts, vacations to the mountains for skiing or river rafting and movies. We spent hours shopping for make-up and underwear for dates I was now actually going on. We had late-night phone calls to update each other on our quest to find Mr. Right. She was a single mother with two young girls to care for, but she always found time for me. She welcomed me as part of her family.

Down went the books and the numbers on the scale. I learned to love and take care of myself. I left that self-imposed prison to which I had sentenced myself. Within a year, I had the courage to leave a dead-end, yet safe job and move to Mississippi, where I knew no one.

For many friends, distance has a way of ending all bonds, and I thought it would be the same for us. My friend insisted we could make it work. Through the magic of instant messaging and daily phone calls; it actually did.

Her illness came on suddenly after a trip to Florida. She was tired on vacation. We thought it was because of too much sun, playing with the kids for hours in the ocean or even possibly the desserts she insisted we eat before the start of every meal. But it wasn't. Within two weeks of returning from our trip, she was no longer able to work. Her colon had shut down, followed by her bladder. By summer's end, she was placed on oxygen, passed out several times a day and sometimes needed a wheelchair. By fall, I vowed to drive up every weekend to help.

She flew to California to her mom's house to see if doctors there could help. After six weeks, she was no closer to being cured than she had been in Tennessee. Finally, the following year, we had a diagnosis: an autoimmune disease with a life expectancy of three to seven years.

The news was heartbreaking. But somehow, despite almost always being bed-ridden and in constant pain, my friend's life was still filled with laughter. Yes, the talks about Mr. Right for both of us stopped and even traveling more than a few hours was out of the question.

But we still had a good time.

Now, our weekends were filled with different plans. We watched movies and Lifetime television. We made late night runs for Strawberry Cheesecake Blizzards.

We watched the girls take their first tentative steps into the dating world. We commiserated with them over their boyfriends. Insomnia was part of the disease. Sometimes we would talk all night. We discussed our future trips, where we would go and who we would meet. We planned sky and scuba diving excursions, what we would wear on the beach and ordering room service. We both knew it would never happen but liked the fantasy anyway.

My friend's illness became much worse, and worry began to weigh us down. In the end, it was just her family and me. Everyone else eventually stopped calling, helping or even dropping by for a short visit. It was too hard to handle and a big slap of reality in the face for most people.

How much longer can she take care of herself? How much more can her body stand? we asked ourselves. But my friend's answer was always the same, "Don't worry. I'm going to be fine."

But she wasn't fine. And in December 2003, she slipped away at home in her bedroom while the girls were asleep.

At the funeral, everyone I met kept repeating the same phrase. "You were so good to her — the best friend anyone could have." But oh, how they were wrong. You see, it wasn't me who was the good friend. It was the other way around. My best friend, who had suffered more than anyone I have ever known, taught me to live and laugh again. It was the purest form of friendship and love I have ever known. It's a debt that can never be repaid, and one I shall never forget. It changed my life.

They say time heals all wounds. Sometimes it does not. Grief is no longer my daily companion. But I remain saddened by the loss of someone with such a great capacity to love. But no matter how blue I sometimes still get, I'm fine because my best pal taught me to be that way. And to Traci Oliver, my rescuer and truest friend: Don't forget to always be ready because someday, somehow, I'm coming to get you.

Pop-A-Roos

by Ephie Johnson

Maya Angelou once said, "Nothing will work unless you do." Both my parents, Monroe and JoeAnn Ballard, proved this concept throughout my childhood. My father was a jack-of-all-trades. He was a science teacher during the day. In the evenings and summer, he would take on work to ensure our family had what we needed. Many nights he would weld to make security bars for air conditioners. I would wake up in the middle of the night and see, what I thought was lightning flashing. It would be my dad in the backyard welding. In the summer, when school was out, he would mow lawns, trim trees, and paint houses.

He did what he needed to do to ensure provision for our family. He included us children whenever possible. We weren't eager beavers about it. But my daddy's philosophy was everyone must learn to work and contribute.

No matter what the job was, my siblings and I were there helping, Summertime and weekends... We already knew it was Camp Monroe! If he was cutting a tree, he was telling me how to cut the tree, while he was cutting the tree. Then I had to drag the limbs to the street. He was always teaching, while he was doing.

I'll never forget one summer he got a contract to do landscaping for a law firm. Their offices were on a busy street in my city, so lots of people were driving and walking by. I was 17 years old, and wouldn't you know it, some boys I knew walked by! It wasn't too common for girls to be cutting grass and trimming hedges. I was really embarrassed. But my daddy didn't play, so I had to keep pushing.

Over the years, I learned how to do physical labor. But I also learned about strategy and structure. My father always had a little notepad and a pen in his pocket. He wrote everything down. I learned to do the same thing. If you want to develop consistency, documentation and regimen are key. I've learned over the years if you want your plans to come to pass write them down and refer to them often.

My mother had incredible vision and she was the essence of bold and courageous. My daddy always said, "I'm here to help bring your mother's vision to reality." He trusted her knowledge and innovation. She knew what she needed to do to help the community. She had her own set of life circumstances that prepared her to achieve the work she was called to do.

My mother was a go-getter. She didn't take a lot of time to think about how she was going to get something done. She saw what needed to be done and went to work. Whenever there was a need, she sought a way to get it met. She was ready and willing to lend a hand and make a difference.

One day it dawned on me my children were not growing up in the same environment I did. Everything they've ever known, about our work, was well established before they were born. This includes our family's ministry work and my music and television career. They'd never had to do the work my siblings, and I did growing up.

Now, don't get me wrong. Our boys have seen both my husband and I work hard. They have seen my parent's ministry grow to help countless of children and families in need. But they never saw us start something from the very beginning. They didn't get to see the work from the start. They missed seeing what goes into building something from an idea or personal expression of love or concern for a neighbor in need.

My boys needed something that would teach them the same work ethic I learned a child. I desired for my husband and me to expand on the legacy. We wanted a way to provide jobs to our neighbors in need of one. At the same time, we could create something our immediate family could develop from the ground up.

We tossed around a few ideas on our return from our summer vacation. Then we came up with the idea to open a gourmet popcorn shop.

We often talked about big ideas we would have, and it seemed no different when the popcorn idea came up. As usual, I began to think aloud. I talked about how great an idea this was and said we should go for it. Then one of my sons said something I will never forget.

"Mom, you're never going to do it. You talk about things you want to do, like this, all the time and you never do them." That hit me like a ton of bricks. Life is short, so I couldn't keep delaying the lessons I wanted to teach my boys by keeping the dreams and ideas in my head.

Those words were the fuel I needed to act. It was just a couple of months later in October 2014, when we opened Pop-A-Roos Gourmet Popcorn Shoppe. The old-fashioned charm of the name, coupled with great tasting popcorn and customer service became our hallmark.

It was hard in the beginning. We didn't have all the proper equipment. We didn't have the recipes to make my own popcorn. We didn't have the experience. There was a lot of trial and error and because I was the primary visionary. I burned myself more times than I can count on that old popcorn machine my dad left us. I didn't have a clue about what I was doing. It took time and advice from a few mentors along the way, but eventually, we started producing our own flavors.

The kids were in school, and my husband works at a University, so it was up to me to push forward. I would go to the shop early in the morning before work, two to three days a week to make the popcorn. Then our one employee would sell the popcorn throughout the day. This was what we had to do to make it work. That's how it is when you are running your own business. You are responsible for everything.

The work ethic of my parents resonated each time I woke up before the sun rose. Many days I'd have to be at work by 8 o'clock, so everything had to be done before then.

I would put on some old clothes and an old wig, roll up my sleeves and get to work. When I finished making all the popcorn for the day, I went to work.

I would head to the restroom, shower, put on my good wig and dress for my job. I am the President and CEO of the nonprofit Neighborhood Christian Centers, Incorporated. We provide programs and services for over 50,000 neighbors in need. I was determined that my son's words would never come to pass.

Both of these roles were important to me. Both roles required focus and dedication, but some days I wanted just to say, "OK, we tried it. Let's stop now."

My father and mother both taught me to keep God at the forefront and acknowledge Him in everything I do. I knew we couldn't quit.

Now, my sons are older, and they have seen what it takes to make things work. They've spent summers working at the Shoppe and setting up stations for events. We have demonstrated to them you do what you have to do to bring your dream to pass.

If food or sleep becomes your god, it may be quite difficult for you to move past your present circumstances. You must stretch yourself and sacrifice to move you into a vision you can see.

My prayer is that I have passed on many of the lessons my parents taught me to my children. I pray my husband and I have taught them new ones as well.

My parents sacrificed and set the example on building a legacy. My family and I now work to continue to build on that foundation for our children and their future.

My father's dying words to us children were, "Know YOUR business." So we work hard every day to stay focused on the work, the business he has called us to do and to stick together as a family. Daily my personal goal is to carry on my parents' legacy and work ethic. I know I am who I am today because of them and the grace of God.

I am grateful my son's words activated and motivated me to bring the dream into reality. Proverbs 14:23 says "All hard work brings a profit, but mere talk leads only to poverty." Who knew I would learn such a valuable lesson from my children teaching them a lesson of my own.

Reach the Finish Line

by Almetria Turner

"For the image you see in the mirror is one of God's masterpieces. He makes no mistakes!"

All the warning signs were there screaming at me. I ignored them. The doctors told me something needed to change. But I told myself, "Soon." I convinced myself I would make changes tomorrow or next week. Soon never came. Weeks turned into months and months turned into years. Until one day, I stepped on the scale and the number staring back at me could not be ignored. That number spoke to me in a way nothing else had up to this point.

342. That was the magic number on the scale. It was also the number that stood in the way of me living a healthy, fulfilling and abundant life.

I struggled to be healthy my entire life. My. Entire. Life. I ate my way through life. I felt like food was my faithful friend. It provided comfort, happiness and solace during the lowest as well as the highest moments in my life. I was an emotional eater.

In 2009, I developed Type 2 Diabetes. I was diagnosed with hypertension years before. That summer, I visited three different specialists. I saw an endocrinologist, cardiologist and a pulmonary specialist. I also saw my primary care physician for several health scares.

Self-hatred and depression plagued me. I often wondered how I could do this to myself. I was going through life existing rather than living it.

I was in denial for the longest time about my life, the condition I was in and chronic illnesses. Being overweight, diabetic, hypertensive and somewhat depressed was a dangerous game. I was a ticking time bomb of potentially catastrophic health problems. Grace and mercy followed me. I knew my time was running out because I was slowly killing myself. I was given chance after chance and only had one shot left. I knew I had to do something about it.

I started my weight loss and fitness journey after being sick and tired of being sick and tired.

It was my goal to become healthy, fit and medication-free by the time I turned 40. "Fit by Forty!" became my new mantra.

I changed my mindset, eating habits and relationship with food. I moved from being sedentary to physically active. I went to various exercise and workout classes. I walked daily, but often wondered if I ever could become a runner. So, I decided to give it a try. I struggled at first and wanted to quit many times. With each run, I found a new appreciation of nature, life and the love it gave me.

When I first began my weight loss journey, running was never part of the equation. Running gave me freedom. I embraced the sacred pavement. I realized how running transformed my life and the lessons I learned. I finally understood I was inspiring others to start somewhere as I had been inspired the same way by so many along the way.

It doesn't matter if I am going for a casual run or competing in a race, I will never get to run or cross that place in time again. While I'm out there, I want to run free and make every second count. My life has completely changed in the last seven years. I had suitcases for emotional, mental, spiritual and physical problems. They were weighing me down. I dropped the baggage I carried for so much of my life.

As of today, I have lost 177 pounds and I am medication-free. I reversed my diabetes and no longer have hypertension. I went from being a size 32 to a size 6-8. Best of all, I am fit and finally free.

As an avid runner, I've completed every major distance of a race except for an ultra. An ultra is when you run anything more than 26.2 miles.

My weight loss story has been featured in many media outlets and publications such as the Huffington Post, Women's Running Magazine, Redbook Magazine, and Yahoo Health.

I appeared on NBC's Today show. I shared my weight loss story, success secrets and healthy recipes as a part of their Joy Fit Club segment.

I plan on doing more of what makes me happy; things I was afraid to do out of fear. I've had numerous opportunities to touch more lives through working with different organizations and meeting new people.

I am the founder of Fit and Finally Free, a food and fitness blog dedicated to help people adopt a healthier and holistic lifestyle by sharing stories, recipes, and teaching them how to shop, cook and eat healthy on a budget. I am also a motivational speaker, published author, as well as a lifestyle, wellness and certified running coach.

When one discovers their passion in life, a sense of purpose manifests and doors begin to open. My pain has become my purpose and my purpose has become my national platform.

I grew up as a poor, overweight little girl. I was born to a single parent. I never imagined my life would turn out in such a magnificent way because I didn't think I could thrive after experiencing so much pain. But I'm still here.

I'm in a position to help so many others who are in still in the fight and running for their lives. The race is not given to the swift nor to the strong, but to the one who endures the end. I want to see people not give up by helping them make it to the end.

Life is a marathon and not a sprint. I'm looking forward to seeing how the rest of my life will unfold as I'm running toward the finish line and I'm handed my medal with the inscription on the back that says, "Well done, good and faithful servant."

In the Blink of an Eye

by Mignonne Wright

I first met Katrina in Fort Lauderdale, Florida. It was August 25, 2005, when she roared ashore only miles from our hotel. I was there on business; desperately trying to get to a safe place. My van was blowing from lane to lane on the interstate, just two hours before Katrina made landfall. It was my first and hopefully last hurricane. And since everything is relative, I thought it was pretty intense. Four days later, we all watched in horror as a much angrier Katrina laid waste to the Gulf Coast in the blink of an eye.

Like almost everyone, I wanted to help. Part of me felt guilty for making it through unscathed. Another part was drawn to the victims of the flooded towns in Louisiana and Mississippi because of the near drowning of my daughter just a month earlier.

Katrina eventually blew her way up to Tennessee. She had weakened significantly, but the wind and rain were still strong enough to wake up my children. When I went to bed that night to the sound of Katrina pounding on my door, I wondered about the people who had no homes, no beds, no pillows. As I closed my eyes, I knew it was the last evening I would spend wondering about their welfare. I met them for the first time just 24 hours later.

I prayed to God and told him I was going to travel south to help. The news reports said all the gas was out south of

Jackson, Mississippi. I prayed, "God, I will drive south as long as I have gas. You can let me know how far you want me to go by providing it for us."

I grabbed a friend, rented a van and loaded it with supplies. We packed water, food, T-shirts, toilet paper and feminine products. We knew these items would be in short supply. I vowed to drive as long as we had fuel. And drive we did.

Just four days after the hurricane hit — before the military arrived in New Orleans – we traveled through Mississippi, to Hattiesburg, Waveland, Bay St. Louis and Pass Christian. Then we headed into Louisiana through Slidell, Laplace, and Kenner. God ended up taking us all the way to the New Orleans airport. He provided for us the entire way. Most stations were entirely out of gas and had hundreds of cars waiting in line for it to arrive. We always managed to find what we needed just when we needed it. So we kept going.

Our first stop was at a Red Cross shelter in Hattiesburg at 2:00 AM. That's when reality hit. The victims were no longer just images on television. People were sleeping on a concrete floor, and it was eerily calm. The head of the shelter told me they needed T-shirts, so we left two boxes and went back to the van to sleep. The next morning, we drove further south with no clear plan, except to stay out of the way while helping as many people as possible.

As we approached interstate 90 in Waveland, Mississippi, time stood still. Kmart was on our left, and the damage was obvious. There was a hand-painted sign announcing the parking lot as "Camp Katrina." It was there that many of the towns' residents were now living.

There were tents made of sheets and garbage bags with bits of tape holding them together. As we drove through the parking lot, one woman ran up to our car frantically asking for a medic. Others just stared off into the distance, and I found myself asking, "Where am I?" It was like a bad dream and entirely unexpected. These people were struggling just to survive.

I imagined the cars in the parking lot must have been like autumn leaves, in a wind of water, dancing as Katrina wrapped her arms around the town. Families were roaming the streets with all of their belongings in grocery carts. We offered food and water to a young couple with two small children. They politely declined, explaining they had a few bottles left and a little food. They directed us to some people down the road who had nothing.

We continued east to where the bridge was out in Bay St. Louis. Climbing through the debris of one woman's house we helped to gather bits and pieces of her life. We found waterlogged photos from long ago – black-and-white pictures of the elderly woman's children. She wanted to talk about her family, and we patiently listen to her stories – hoping we were offering some sense of normalcy as we stood in the ruins of her home. We climbed through the debris to retrieve her computer hard drive for her since bulldozers were getting ready to come through. We left her talking to a young rescue worker who was offering her help to a shelter. She hugged us and thanked us for our help.

Next, we headed to Slidell. At a relief station for rescue workers, volunteers were cooking steaks from the freezer of a local steakhouse. The city had no power, and the windows were all shattered at the restaurant. Somebody got the great idea to go in and get all the steaks out of their freezer before they spoiled. We gave them water, T-shirts and hard candies. One of the young men was cooking for the police. He had been carried away by the storm surge and was thankful for a new shirt to wear. Although he had to swim to survive, he was now laughing and smiling as he commanded the large grill. They invited us to stay and eat, but we explained we were heading toward New Orleans. They wished us luck. As we drove away, I glanced in the rearview mirror and saw them smiling and waving.

We approached the first barricade on interstate 55 heading into New Orleans. When the Highway Patrol Officers at the roadblock stopped us, we offered them water, coffee and peanut butter crackers. They decided to let us pass since our supplies were needed in New Orleans. We made it through two more barricades before we found ourselves completely alone, driving over Lake Pontchartrain.

We were a bit shocked we had made it this far. We were listening to CNN on satellite radio, continuously hearing reports of the chaos in the city. My heart started beating faster. Although nervous, our need to help was greater than our fear. We continued. We drove past scores of news trucks as we headed to the airport. All the big boys were there—CNN, NBC, ABC. It was getting way too real. What lay ahead? As it turned out, it was nothing like we expected.

There was no hysteria, no violence—just thousands of families, crammed shoulder to shoulder as far as you could see. Yes, they were tired and dirty but also calm. And despite the horrific events they experienced—these were the people who lived in the Superdome for five days—many were smiling, laughing or trying to help. It was as if the floodwaters had washed away all barriers. There were no rich or poor, no old or young, no black or white: just people, happy to be alive.

There were so many incidences of kindness by those who lost so much or too many to count. One man we met couldn't find his mother or daughter. He thought they might be in Dallas, but he wasn't sure. When offered a ride to Houston on one of the large buses headed that way, he immediately turned it down, saying others have been waiting much longer.

Another woman dressed in hospital scrubs had no shoes. She was rescued from the top of her car by a helicopter, evacuated to a hospital and then to the airport. She asked if I could go to Walgreens and buy her a pair of shoes, not understanding that there were no longer any drugstores. I offered my own pair of sandals, but she turned them down three times. She finally took them after I said, "When you get back on your feet, you can do something nice for someone else." She started to cry and hugged me as she put my shoes on. When the military began bringing in MRE's (meals ready to eat) we left to find others who needed our supplies. It wasn't long before we found them.

We traveled south until we couldn't drive any further. There was no more road, and rescue workers from the South Carolina Department of Natural Resources were launching boats. We stopped and offered them coffee in self-heating cans. They were so excited — no one had tasted coffee in days. We gave them all we had. "It's like liquid gold," one rescue worker said.

We headed out to pass Christian. We drove all the way to the beach and stared at what was once a beautiful seaside town. But there was nothing left – no people, no houses, no school. All that remained were reminders of everyday life: a teddy bear, a child's bed and a doghouse in the middles of the road. I wondered who these items belonged to. Did they make it out? Were they safe? Had they found shelter? I said a silent prayer on the beach for all those who had suffered through this horrible tragedy.

With no one to help, we headed back to Hattiesburg. In less than 12 hours, there were three times as many people at the shelter, and it was quickly running out of supplies. People everywhere were wearing the T-shirts we dropped off the previous evening, from nurses to evacuees who helped us unload the rest of our supplies. One of the doctors came outside, threw her arms around us and repeatedly thanked us. "You don't understand," she said. "These things you brought us – it's all we have."

After one final stop for gas, we headed home. While sitting in the silence, I started to cry. I thought of all I had seen and all of the emotions I felt over the last 24 hours. Our van was now empty. We had nothing left to give – no food, no water and I was barefoot. But I was coming home with a heart full of hope.

I saw people who lost everything, helping one another when all they had left to give was themselves. God brought me on the journey to provide me with the most magnificent view of the human condition. In the darkest of times, these people found a light. They lost so much, but they were incredibly thankful for what they had left. Witnessing this changed my life – in the blink of an eye — of a hurricane named Katrina.

Epilogue

by Roquita Coleman-Williams

Thank you for taking this journey with us. Twenty-two women, 22 stories; from hospital bed breakthroughs to serving "liquid gold" in the aftermath of the severest storm.

Among these pages, I hope you found a story that gives you hope. Perhaps, you simply needed to know you are not alone in what feels like a rough transformation from a chunk of coal to a diamond.

The common element between coal and diamonds is carbon. Let the difficulties and challenges of your life be your carbon. Take the lessons and wisdom from your struggles and allow them to polish you into the most- precious, brilliant element.

What will be your carbon? Is it surrender, truth, transparency, faith or optimism. What will take you from the darkness to the light?

We are more than characters in a walking motion picture.

Despair will not make you a victim.

Violation will not make your villain.

Being silenced will not make you a bystander.

You are the healer, hero and leader in your life. Whether you let peace be your umpire or you claim success after failure, you will find the best version of yourself through the moments that challenge you the most.

Lift your head above those that laugh at your dreams. Let the laughter fuel you to Dream in color and To dream out loud!

And when life devastates you, know that you can simply pick up a phone and whisper a prayer. If you are battling with your self-confidence, take a look in the mirror and proclaim "I can achieve anything I put my mind to for I am fearless and I'm beautiful." You can love yourself. You can be real and authentic and you can turn your "mess into your message"!

Anxiety will not win.

Abuse will not win.

Self-doubt will not win.

Infidelity will not win.

Humiliation will not win.

Loss will not win.

Heartache will not win.

Illness will not win.

Addiction will not win.

Forgiveness is your carbon.

Respect is your carbon.

Love is your carbon.

Boundaries are your carbon.

Serving others is your carbon.

Acceptance is your carbon.

Grace is your carbon.

It is your time to live your life in total freedom. I hope the stories we have courageously shared inspire you to claim your diamond!

Meet the Contributors

Natasha Donerson is a Business Development expert, published author, and professional speaker. With over 20 years of business experience as a sales and marketing executive, real estate investing, and entrepreneur, she drives results. Natasha earned her B.S. from Spelman College and her MBA from Union University. She serves on the Economic Development Growth Engine Board for Shelby County in Tennessee. She has served on the Board of St Francis Hospital-Bartlett, TN, Memphis Chamber of Commerce, Bartlett Chamber of Commerce, and Memphis Chapter of the National Association of Women Business Owners. The Memphis Business Journal selected her as a Top 40 under 40 Honoree and Super Woman in Business. She is also a member of Alpha Kappa Alpha Sorority. Natasha is the proud mom of one daughter, Naomi.

Mrs. Erica Stiff-Coopwood, Esq. is a native of Yazoo City. Erica received her Bachelor of Arts in Psychology, with Honor, from Agnes Scott College. In 2000, Erica went on to attend Vanderbilt University Law School where she earned her Juris Doctorate. In her life as an attorney, Erica served as a law clerk on the Tennessee Supreme Court; and as an employment law defense litigator. Erica is the first Black president of the Junior League of Memphis. Most notably, Erica has seen God's hand work very meticulously with her as a wife and mom. She and her husband Reginald Coopwood, have five beautiful and (mostly) obedient children: Reginald II, Ryan, Reuben, and Riley Nicole and Rebecca Anne.

Rose Jackson Flenorl is a manager in the internationally-recognized FedEx Global Citizenship group. She leads a team of professionals committed to representing the heart of the corporation. Her team focuses on executing strategic programs and maintaining relationships with national and international non-profit organizations. Rose has more than 30 years of experience in marketing, communications and corporate social responsibility. A graduate of the University of Mississippi, she was the first black female named to the student Hall of Fame and was chosen by Glamour Magazine as one of the top 10 college women in the United States. In 2008 she served as president of the National Alumni Association, and in 2015-16 she served as the board chair of the University of Mississippi Foundation.

Emily Harvey is a graphic designer working out of her art studio in Midtown Memphis, Tennessee. She continues to raise awareness of the opioid epidemic among other women who have lost loved ones to overdose. Learn more about the Phone of the Spirit at www.phoneofthespirit.org. See Emily's artwork at www.emkatdesign.com.

Jae Henderson is an author, speaker and entrepreneur living in Memphis, TN. She enjoys encouraging others to live their best life while improving their community. To read more works by Jae, visit www.jaehendersonauthor.com.

Natasha Nassar Hazlett is a coach, inspirational speaker, and author of the best-selling book Unstoppable Influence: Be You. Be Fearless. Transform Lives. She empowers entrepreneurs around the world with the clarity, confidence, and strategies they need to boost their income and influence while working less, by monetizing their message online. In addition to being a mentor and coach, Natasha is an award-winning internet marketer, attorney, and the co-founder of Fast Forward Marketing, LLC with her husband Rich. Together they are on a mission to help people find and follow their life's purpose. Of all the titles she holds, her favorite is "mommy" to an adorable little girl who is the light of her life. You can find Natasha at her blog: NatashaHazlett.com.

Meredith Johnson of Lafayette, LA is a poet, writer, public speaker and businesswoman. She earned her degree in Cultural Anthropology at ULL. Johnson is fluent in French and enjoys learning about and experiencing world cultures. She is currently working on her memoir, A Map to Hell and Back, which chronicles her journey living with Bipolar II Disorder. Johnson plans to travel around the country, facilitating speaking tours around her book, and helping others who are still suffering from the disease. She enjoys writing, traveling, hiking, and dancing.

Pamela Williams Kelly, Esq. is the mother of three sons and one daughter. She is an attorney who practices immigration, entertainment and family law. Pamela earned her Bachelor of Arts degree in Communications from Mississippi State University and her Juris Doctor degree from The University of Memphis School of Law. Pamela has experience in radio promotions, human resources and worked as a teacher at Westwood High School and as an adjunct professor at Strayer

University, Remington College and The University of Phoenix. Pamela volunteers to prevent domestic violence, improve literacy, provide free/ low-cost legal services and mentor high school and college students.

Nikkya Hargrove is the Program Director for a non-profit called Harboring Hearts. She works each day to help pediatric and adult heart surgery patients with their financial and emotional needs. She does this by providing emergency housing support and other critical resources. Nikkya and her wife, who is a hospital chaplain, are raising their three kids in the New England area. She is also a freelance writer with work featured in Elle, The Washington Post, Shondaland and others. When Nikkya is not working or running after her three children, she finds peace in the quiet of a bookstore, coffee shop, or being with her wife.

Pat Morgan has worked for more than three decades to help homeless people break the cycle of homelessness. Now retired, she continues to be a relentless advocate and volunteer, working with homeless people and professionals to help improve the "system" of services and housing. An accomplished writer, her first book, "The Concrete Killing Fields, which has won five national awards, tells the story of some of her homeless friends and her wildly impossible, wildly successful journey to live out her "calling" and her dreams. She loves spending quality time with her family and friends, the outdoors, long walks along the Mississippi River, music, sports, reading, and writing. You can learn more about Pat and her work at www.patmorganauthor.com

Debrena Jackson Gandy is a nationally published best-selling author of three books, a highly sought-after keynote speaker, transformational life coach, relationships mentor and guest blogger, and life coach specializing in personal growth and spiritual development. She's been seen on TV on CNN, CNN Live, and Good Day New York, and in Oprah's O, Essence, Ebony, and Day. She is a former TV show host for TBN. She lives in Seattle with her fabulous husband and their three amazing daughters. All things Debrena can be found at www.MillionDollarMentor.net

Siobhan Riley (pronounced Shavon) works in State Representative Antonio Parkinson's office. She is currently over media and community relations. She was previously a TV news reporter for ten years. She worked at WREG in Memphis, WJRT in Flint Michigan and WCBI in Columbus, Mississippi where she received the Mississippi Associated Press Award. Siobhan started her career in Gainesville, Florida at WCJB. She grew up in Greensboro, North Carolina. She graduated Summa Cum Laude from North Carolina A&T State University with her BA in Journalism and Mass Communication. There, she received the "Most Outstanding Graduate Award" in the journalism department. Siobhan is the former president of the Memphis Association of Black Journalists. Currently, she serves as the chair of the National Association of Black Journalists Council of Presidents.

Marilynn Sasportas Robinson is a native New Yorker. She received her BA degree, cum laude, from Harvard-Radcliffe College, and her Master of Public Health from the Yale School

150

of Public Health. Recently retired, she served as Senior Vice President at Saint Francis Healthcare. In addition, she co-pastored St. Andrew AME Church along with her husband. A 13-year breast cancer survivor, Rev. Marilynn is an advocate for women's health services and a sought-after speaker. She's an active community volunteer in the Memphis area. Yet, she is most passionate about working with children on Saturdays at a community library she founded in 2010. Joyfully married since 1979, the Robinsons have been blessed with a set of identical, twin daughters—Maisha Tamar and Nuriya Desta, both physicians.

Kathryn Vigness is a speaker, author, and life coach. She is a #boymama, yogi, and lover of all things happy. As an avid writer, Kathryn is a featured contributor to multiple online journals and the author of Growing Wild and the inspirational journal, #soulprompt. Kathryn's only goal at the end of her life is to have lived a life serving others. She is a fireproof change agent and a resiliency advocate. She is living proof that life gives us what we always need, not always what envisioned. Keep up with Kathryn on Instagram at @kvigness or find her at kathrynvigness.com

Jasmine "Jaz" Gray is a storyteller, social entrepreneur and researcher from Memphis, TN. She speaks on a range of topics including healthy self-image, rare disease/patient experience, bullying and resilience. Her first short film, Ryan's Story, premiered at the Chinese Theatre in Hollywood, CA. Her non-profit Jaz's Jammies Inc. has donated over 6,000 pairs of new pajamas to sick/homeless children. Jaz has worked for publications including the Nashville Tennessean and media companies including Paramount Pictures where she co-founded an ad-hoc committee to address health-related diversity. In addition to a B.S. from Middle Tennessee State University and an M.A. from Syracuse University, she is currently pursuing a Ph.D. at UNC Chapel Hill. Jaz is motivated to use every gift and opportunity to glorify God and uplift people's lives.

Amy Speropoulos graduated from the University of Alabama with a degree in Broadcast Communications. Her first on-air TV Job was during her senior year at Alabama. From there she skipped across the South, then to Missouri and in 1999 settled in Memphis. Amy's worked at three out of four Memphis stations and is still in good standing with them all. While at WREG she met her husband, Scott, fell in love and they now have three little girls. WATN came calling unexpectedly and offered Amy her own show. She's having a ball. Amy now spends an hour each day talking about the city she loves, the people she cares about, the history and heritage in which she is deeply entwined.

Sherica Hymes is the founder and CEO of Polished Consulting, LLC and the Total Woman Summit. She has the heart for serving, and people are her passion. She and her team specialize in strategic execution, executive coaching, organizational development, developing high performing teams and leading large-scale organizational change. As a motivational speaker, she captivates audiences as a gifted storyteller and orator. She serves on several Boards, and her company is a certified Small Business and Minority Business

Enterprise. Her greatest role is being a mom. She is a woman of faith and truly believes that "to whom much is given, much is truly required." Sherica knows our lives must be lived in such a way, that our presence is felt long after we have physically departed.

Amy Lorton is senior writer for Ramsey Solutions in Nashville, Tenn. She also is the founder of CopyWrite Media and the former editor of Chicken Soup of the Soul Magazine. Go to copywritemedia.com to learn more.

Ephie Johnson is the President and CEO of the Neighborhood Christian Centers, Inc. She is a business owner, Life Coach, Consultant, Professional Speaker and Vocalist. She is married and has 2 Children. To learn more about her life and work you are invited to visit her website www.EphieJohnsonLive.com.

Almetria Turner is a Wellness Coach, Food and Fitness Blogger, RRCA Certified Running Coach, Published Author and Motivational Speaker who inspires and educates people on how to live a healthier lifestyle. She was featured on NBC's, "The Today Show," the national running publication, "Women's Running Magazine and many others for her 177-pound weight loss, overcoming diabetes, hypertension and how running saved her life.

Mignonne Wright is a nationally award-winning executive with over 20 years of experience. Forbes named her a digital influencer and creative marketing "guru." She is a dedicated entrepreneur, avid community partner and philanthropist.

Mignonne has been honored by The New York Times and Media Industry News as one of the most intriguing people in media, marketing and branding. She was named Top 30 Under 30 by AdAge and Top 40 Under 40 by the Memphis Business Journal. Mignonne is a founding member of Young Women in Philanthropy. She has served on several boards focusing on various issues such as education, economic diversity, animal rights and historic preservation to name a few. Her most important project to date is focusing on faith and helping others to learn more about her favorite subject, God!

To contribute a story to the next
book in the *Storealities* series
go to Storealities.com.